CONGRATULATIONS
GOD
BELIEVES
IN YOU!

Books by Lloyd J. Ogilvie

12 STEPS TO LIVING WITHOUT FEAR
THE OTHER JESUS
IF GOD CARES, WHY DO I STILL HAVE PROBLEMS?
MAKING STRESS WORK FOR YOU
ACTS, VOL. 5, COMMUNICATOR'S COMMENTARY
CONGRATULATIONS, GOD BELIEVES IN YOU!
THE BUSH IS STILL BURNING
WHEN GOD FIRST THOUGHT OF YOU
DRUMBEAT OF LOVE
LIFE WITHOUT LIMITS
LET GOD LOVE YOU
THE AUTOBIOGRAPHY OF GOD
JESUS THE HEALER
LONGING TO BE FREE
LOVED AND FORGIVEN
LORD OF THE UPS AND DOWNS
IF I SHOULD WAKE BEFORE I DIE
A LIFE FULL OF SURPRISES
YOU'VE GOT CHARISMA
CUP OF WONDER
GOD'S BEST FOR MY LIFE
THE RADIANCE OF INNER SPLENDOR
GIFT OF FRIENDSHIP
GIFT OF LOVE
GIFT OF CARING
GIFT OF SHARING

CONGRATULATIONS GOD BELIEVES IN YOU!

CLUES TO HAPPINESS FROM THE BEATITUDES

LLOYD J. OGILVIE

WORD BOOKS
PUBLISHER
WACO, TEXAS

ISBN 0-8499-2994-6
Library of Congress catalog card number: 80-53249
Printed in the United States of America

89801239 RRD 98765432

CONTENTS

Introduction   7

1. I Just Want to Be Happy   11
    *"And seeing the multitudes, He went up on a
    mountain, and when He was seated His disciples
    came to Him. And He opened His mouth and
    taught them saying, 'Blessed . . .'" (Matt. 5:1–2)*

2. Down the Corridors of Our Need   21
    *"Blessed are the poor in spirit,
    For theirs is the kingdom of heaven." (Matt. 5:3)*

3. Three Words Spell Happiness   31
    *"Blessed are those who mourn,
    For they shall be comforted." (Matt. 5:4)*

4. The Door to Happiness Has Two Keys   47
    *"Blessed are the gentle,
    For they shall inherit the earth." (Matt. 5:5)*

5. The Happiness of a Consuming Passion   61
    *"Blessed are those who hunger and
    thirst for righteousness,
    For they shall be filled." (Matt. 5:6)*

6. Happiness Is Your Pain in My Heart   77
    *"Blessed are the merciful,
    For they shall obtain mercy." (Matt. 5:7)*

7. Happiness Is Having Eyes in Your Heart   87
    "Blessed are the pure in heart,
    For they shall see God." (Matt. 5:8)

8. The First Steppers   99
    "Blessed are the peacemakers,
    For they shall be called the sons of God." (Matt. 5:9)

9. A Daring Friendship   113
    "Blessed are those who are persecuted
    for righteousness' sake,
    For theirs is the kingdom of heaven." (Matt. 5:10)

10. I Believe in You   125
    "You are the salt of the earth . . .
    You are the light of the world." (Matt. 5:13–14)

INTRODUCTION

Everyone wants to be happy. But what is happiness? I've spent years collecting people's definitions. They all have one thing in common. Happiness for most people is considered to be the cumulative result of getting what we want. It's acquiring our heart's desire, possessing our dreams. And yet, I observe that often when people get what they thought they wanted, they are still not happy. Could the problem be that we wanted too little? Is our idea of happiness pitched far too low?

I believe we must return to the Author of Life to discover the secret of what true happiness was meant to be. In the Beatitudes, Jesus Christ radically reorients our goals, values, and hopes. He gives us the eightfold mystery of happiness. Each of the Beatitudes reveals an aspect of the quality of life which brings lasting happiness. The Beatitudes are the Master's Magna Carta of a truly happy life. The happiness He offers is rooted in grace, nurtured in profound joy, and expressed in our daily life and relationships. Happiness is the outer expression of the inner experience of grace-oriented joy. It is knowing we are loved unreservedly and forgiven unconditionally. The Beatitudes help us grasp the reality of that assurance. They tell us what we can be and do to know and experience a profound intimacy with God that will give us a happiness the world or the people of our lives can neither give nor take away.

The Beatitudes are like an overture to an opera They state the basic themes of the Lord's entire teaching. Here is the distilled essence of a distinctly different and higher level of life. Here is Christ's self-portrait for us to behold. His life is incarnated in the Beatitudes; His death defeated the forces of evil which debilitate them; His resurrection presence with us enables us to live them. The life of true happiness our Lord envisioned for us is the life He wants to live in us.

It is significant to me that the Beatitudes are Jesus' first formal teaching after the wilderness temptation. He had done battle with Satan's facsimile of happiness. Each of the temptations—to change stones into bread, to cast Himself down from the Temple, and to acquire the kingdoms of the world for worshiping Satan—were confronted and rejected. The false goals of happiness, then and now, are represented in the immediate, the expedient, and the temporary. When Jesus had battled and won, He was ready to share His secret of happiness, which was so much more than material satisfaction, fame, fortune, and power. The carefully worded, power-packed wisdom of the Beatitudes is truth tempered by the fires of experience. Not a word is wasted in the description of the blessed life He came to reveal. Here is refined gold ready to be excavated and used as the priceless coinage for the abundant life.

A perplexing question sent me back to the Beatitudes. Why are so few people happy? And beneath that observation was a deeper query. Why are so many Christians unhappy? The wants and desires of our idea of happiness hit wide of the mark of Jesus' eightfold revelation of happiness in the Beatitudes. Many of us believe in Christ as Savior and Lord, but His quality of happiness eludes us. A penetrating study of the Beatitudes rewards us with a whole new set of priorities which alone can prepare us to experience the blessedness of profound happiness.

It was this quest of the essence of true happiness that lured me back to the Mount of Beatitude above the Sea of Galilee where Jesus delivered the Sermon on the Mount. During a prolonged study leave devoted to digging out the matchless jewels of the Sermon on the Mount, I would go to the Mount of Beatitude each day to spend hours in prayer, study, and reflection. The Italian nuns of the convent there graciously allowed me to set up a temporary desk in the lovely garden they maintain so faithfully. Each Beatitude became the focus of days of thought and writing. I knew that in my previous teaching and preaching of the Beatitudes I had only scratched the surface. Now I was determined to press deeper, grappling with the seeming paradox each one presented. Picturing the Master teaching there, the disciples at His feet, I listened with mind and heart. And then the fresh springs began to flow.

I was gripped by the startling realization that the Beatitudes are really congratulatory affirmations. The Lord is affirming our real desires beneath our mixed motives and inconsistent performances. He is introducing us to ourselves—the true persons in us who struggle to realize our full potentials. Then it hit me. The Lord is saying, "Congratulations to the real you. I want you to know, love, and release the imprisoned person in you who longs to live. I believe in you!"

My prayer is that the eightfold way to blessed happiness will open up to you in a new way. It leads to the heart of God and then back into our hearts. Uncontainable, unquenchable happiness will radiate from your life and be experienced in your relationships and responsibilities.

I am very thankful to Katherine Guzman for her faithful typing and retyping of the manuscript. These chapters were preached on television and then revised. I am gratified by the fact that so many found the secret of true happiness as they exchanged their inadequate goals which had not brought them happiness and adopted the Master's octagonal offer. I pray for nothing less for you.

Lloyd John Ogilvie

I
JUST
WANT TO
BE HAPPY

"And seeing the multitudes, He went up on a mountain, and when He was seated His disciples came to Him. And He opened His mouth and taught them saying, 'Blessed . . .'"

What do you want out of life?

I've asked people that question thousands of times over the years. With very few exceptions, the response is, "I just want to be happy!"

That answer begs further questions. What do you mean by happy? What is happiness for you? What would it take to make you truly happy?

The replies almost always involve people, places, or things. Happiness for most of us is made up of the who, where, and what of life. It is inseparably related to others, being loved and appreciated, feeling secure, living in the right house, having what we want, working at a satisfying job, and reaching our goals. Being happy is a transitory, circumstantial, person-oriented thing for most. A come-and-go, up-and-down, illusive condition, dependent on the conditions around us and the attitudes of the people with whom we live and associate. We assume that something or someone has the responsibility to make us happy.

And yet, we've all had disturbing moments of truth when we have realized that what we have accumulated, accomplished, and achieved has not made us happy. The alarming realization is intensified by the observation that countless others who have possessions, positions, and power are no more happy than we are. "What's the matter with me?" we ask ourselves. "Why am I not happy with all that I have?"

A few months ago, a man hit me with a disturbing question. "Whatever happened to happiness? We all want it; we talk a lot about it; we are in a mad scramble for it; and yet, there are so few really happy people."

The question has rumbled about in my mind. It has prompted me to think deeply about why so few people are happy.

Get in touch with your real feelings. Are you happy? If so, why? Will it last? If not, why not? What change would make you completely happy? If you received the longings of your heart, would you be happy? If you arrived at where you are going, would you have happiness? And then, the litmus question—what could have the power to diminish or destroy it?

Coupled with our concern over our own fleeting experiences of happiness is our worry over the unhappiness of so many people we know and love. We ache inside when life's problems and disappointments rob loved ones and friends of a happy heart. We want to step in and arrange their happiness. But we cannot give away what we do not have. All the glib, facile slogans about how to be happy clog our throats.

Often we want to give people things or opportunities for pleasure to make them happy. We forget that none of these has made us happy. Like the father who said to his daughter and new son-in-law just before they left on their honeymoon, "Listen, your mother and I have worked hard to provide you two with all the things we never had when we started out. Now, you'd better be happy!" Quite a mandate. You guessed it: the young couple was no happier than the father and mother had been, for all their bequeathed wealth.

The who, what, and where of our idea of happiness is woven into the fiber of American life. Thomas Jefferson wrote into our constitution that we are endowed with certain inalienable rights—life, liberty, and the pursuit of happiness. Our founding father lifted the words right out of the writings of John Locke—with one crucial change. Locke asserted that our inalienable rights were life, liberty, and property. We wonder if property and the pursuit of happiness were synonyms in Jefferson's mind. Whatever the case, the pursuit of happiness is considered the birthright of us Americans—to live, work, strive for it. The limiting legacy remains at the core of our mentality. We think of happiness as something we can capture, acquire, or package as a result of what we do and have.

Happiness is an inside story. It begins inside us, in our hearts. We all long to find the secret of true happiness—a happiness that's unassailable by change, circumstances, or conditions. As one woman put it to me recently, "I want the kind of happiness that lasts—that no discouragement, frustration or grief can destroy."

That's the happiness Jesus Christ came to give us. If we

want to discover true happiness, we must go back to Jesus' springs in His essential message in the Sermon on the Mount. The Beatitudes tell us what authentic happiness is and how to live in its constant flow.

Matthew's introduction in chapter 5 gives us the motive and the method of the Master's message. "And seeing the multitudes, He went up on a mountain, and when He was seated, His disciples came to Him. And He opened His mouth and taught them. . . ." The need in the multitude prompted the Lord's Magna Carta of true happiness. He saw the suffering, anxiety, fear, and worry of the unhappy people. That's why He went up on a mountain and called His disciples. He wanted to give them the secret for the discovery and lasting experience of happiness so that they could multiply His ministry with the multitude and eventually in the world.

He sat down. That denotes an exclamation point. When a rabbi taught something important, he sat down to teach. It was as if Jesus said, "Listen, what I have to say is really crucial. Don't miss a word of it!"

In the same way, we must grapple with and respond to the Master's message. The Lord sees each of us in the multitude and among His disciples. He comprehends with x-ray vision the lack of true happiness in our hearts. What He said then is for us now.

During my daily meditation periods on the Mount of Beatitude I prayed through the meaning of each word, phrase, and sentence of the distilled wisdom of Jesus' way to happiness. As I sat there, I felt His presence and received fresh insight into what He said. I could picture Him seated there, the disciples gathered intently around Him, grasping every word. I felt that I became one of those disciples sitting at His feet and heard the Beatitudes as if for the first time.

The Beatitudes flash with vivid, varied color, blending into the pure white light of the truth about the characteristics of the new breed of humanity Jesus had come to call, commission, and empower. All of the basic themes of the Sermon on the Mount are introduced with impelling intensity. Every one presents us with an aspect of the true meaning of happiness as God intended it to be.

Each of the Beatitudes has three parts: the promise of happiness rooted in blessedness; the key to discovering and experiencing it; and the result in our lives. It follows naturally then that our exposition of the meaning of each Beatitude should be divided into discovering what it means to be blessed in the flashing light of the profound insight each one reveals. Each has a paradox. Only prolonged, prayerful penetration exposes the truth Jesus intended.

Consider first the source of true happiness. It's all wrapped up in this word *blessed*. What does it mean? We must trace it back through the English translations to the original Greek and beyond to the Aramaic in which Jesus spoke. Aramaic was a vernacular kind of Hebrew used in Jesus' day.

The Hebrew word for blessed, *asherē*, is a word of exclamation and congratulation. The meaning is, "O the blessedness of. . . ." In the Old Testament, blessedness was inseparable from the blessing of God. To be blessed was to be a recipient of His blessing. And blessing contained the three powerful ingredients: belonging to God, being His beloved, and brokenness resulting in absolute trust. It means to be called, chosen, loved, forgiven, cherished, and cared for with God's incredible punctuality. This inner experience of God's grace bursts forth in joy throughout the pages of the Old Testament. The blessed of God bless Him in response. The Psalmist

who had a profound experience of the blessing of God
could not contain his joyous praise. "Blessed be the Lord,
for he has wondrously shown his steadfast love to me"
(Ps. 31:21, RSV). The word blessed was also used for a
person who was faithful and obedient. "Blessed is the
man" is the oft-repeated opening of a psalm and ascrip-
tion designating one whose experience of being blessed
resulted in a blessed life.

Thus, we see that the word *blessed* was the special word
of intimacy between God and His people. It was both
summary and synonym for all that God was and had
done for His people. The benediction the Lord gave to
Moses for the blessing of the people through the generations captures the many-splendored dimensions of being
His beloved who belong to Him. ". . . Thus you shall
bless the people of Israel: you shall say to them, The Lord
bless you and keep you: The Lord make his face to shine
upon you, and be gracious to you: The Lord lift up his
countenance upon you, and give you peace. So shall they
put my name upon the people of Israel, and I will bless
them" (Num. 6:22–27, RSV).

All this rich meaning of *blessed* was impacted in Jesus'
use of the word in the Beatitudes. The Greek word used
in the translation of Jesus' original word was *makarios*, an
adjective meaning "happy." Our English word *happy* hits
wide of the mark of the original intention. The Anglo-
Saxon etymology goes back to the root *hap*—meaning
"chance"; thus words like *haply, hapless, happily*. But the
Greek word meant much more than chance. In ancient
Greek literature, the word was used to describe the gods.
It meant sufficiency, satisfaction, security. It is interesting
and illuminating to note that Cypress was called Happy
Isle *(hē makaria)*, because it was self-contained, rich,

fertile, and lovely in and of itself. Happiness in Greek was a divine and godlike joy. Paul used the same Greek adjective for God in his letter to Timothy: "according to the glorious gospel of the blessed [*makariou*, "happy"] God" (1 Tim. 1:11). The happy God is the source of the true happiness of the happy people. Happiness is the adjective of the abundant life Jesus came to offer us. The Beatitudes enumerate the secrets of this abundance.

These secrets are given in the second part of each Beatitude. Initially, they seem to be alarming contradictions of the first part. How can happiness be found in poverty of spirit, mourning, meekness, hungering and thirsting, being merciful, having a pure heart, and making peace? We are as startled as the disciples who first heard the surprising elements of happinesss in Jesus' words. He makes us think, wonder, and then plumb the depths of what He meant. We begin with what seems to be negative and, with His guidance, find the positive He intended. "What did you mean, Lord?" we pray, as we meditate on each Beatitude. His response is winsome: "I hoped you would ask. My truth is never discovered apart from Me. Allow Me to show you." Then, in prayerful fellowship about Him, the realization thunders in our souls. The Beatitudes really describe the Lord Himself! We know what they mean when we know Him and can begin to experience the happiness they offer when He lives in us.

DOWN
THE CORRIDORS
OF
OUR NEED

2

"Blessed are the poor in spirit,
For theirs is the kingdom of heaven."
MATTHEW 5:3

We are shocked when we consider the first secret of
true happiness. The poor in spirit? How can poverty of
spirit bring the blessedness of true happiness?

A quick check on the Greek word used for "poor,"
ptochos, raises further alarm. It means abject poverty, from
ptōssō, "to crouch" or "to cower." That sends us in search
of the Hebrew word for *poor.* Its evolution in Old
Testament usage is less startling and gets us closer to
what Jesus must have meant. The word *ani* in Hebrew
had come to mean more than material poverty. It was
used for the humble and faithful. Thus Psalm 34:4–6: "I
sought the Lord, and he answered me, and delivered me

23

from all my fears. Look to him, and be radiant; so your faces shall never be ashamed. This *poor* man cried, and the Lord heard him, and saved him out of all his troubles" (RSV).

What Jesus meant was that happiness is rooted in humbleness in a person's deep, inner self; his spirit, *pneumatai*. The same word is used in John 4:24. "God is a spirit *(pneuma)*, and those who worship Him must worship Him in spirit *(pneumatai)* and truth." Here Jesus is talking about the invisible and immortal part of us created to respond to and be infused by the Spirit of God. The poor in spirit, the truly humble, can acknowledge their need and cry out for God's help.

The first step to happiness is to cry honestly, "God help me!" The humble-spirited have three sublime qualities: awe, which issues in wonder and praise; realization of need; and receptivity to what God wants to give more than we dare to ask. J. B. Phillips was on the mark when he translated the Beatitude, "How happy are the humble-minded, for the kingdom of heaven is theirs!"

Jesus is congratulating those in whom He found the maturity of true humility. For me, the essence of the first Beatitude is, "O how very happy are those of you who know your need for God, ask Him to help you, and are willing to receive His blessings." Unhappiness is always caused by self-sufficiency which arrogantly demands our making it on our own strength.

The opposite of humility is pride. Spurgeon warned us not to be proud of race, face, or place. The reason is that none of these can make us happy. Pride keeps us from the joy of receiving what God wants to give: Himself. Forgiveness and love. Intimate companionship. C. S. Lewis said, "Pride leads to every other vice: it is the complete anti-God state of mind. Pride is spiritual cancer: it eats up the very possibility of love, or contentment, or even common sense."[1] Self-made people always end up worshiping their maker—themselves!

We become like Aesop's frog who wanted to be as large as the ox and finally exploded. I've often wondered if the fable was the source of Carl Sandburg's alarming observation that "the earth is strewn with the exploded bladders of the puffed up."[2] Why is it that the wrong people usually have the inferiority complexes? Irrelevant question. Pride is the result of the deepest kind of inferiority. It is the sure sign of profound insecurity. Phillips Brooks said, "The true way to be humble is not to stoop until you are smaller than yourself, but to stand at your real height against some higher nature that will show you what the real smallness of your greatness is."[3] Only Jesus Christ can do that for us!

All through His ministry, Jesus commended humility whenever He observed it in human personality. He knew that religious pride was the greatest hindrance to happiness in His beloved nation of Israel. That's why He congratulated the publican and not the Pharisee in His startling parable. The publican who could say, "God be merciful to me," had the poverty of spirit which could provide a breakthrough to God's power. There is no greater need than when we think we have no need. The sickness of the satisfied! It must always be based on a

---

[1]Quoted in Leonard Griffith, *Pathways to Happiness* (Nashville: Abingdon, 1964), p. 24.

[2]In *Living Quotations for Christians*, Sherwood Wirt and Kersten Beckstrom, eds. (New York: Harper and Row, 1974), p. 188.

[3]Ibid., p. 115.

false comparison. "I thank Thee that I am not as other men. . . ." The one thing that the Pharisee could not say was what he needed most to pray: "God, help me!"

Surely that's the reason Jesus made so much of the centurion's pleading request for Him to come heal his servant of paralysis. Unlike many followers of the Master, and in stark contrast to Israel's leaders, the centurion knew his need and believed Jesus could heal his servant. Poverty of spirit cried out for help. And Jesus marveled in commendation: "Assuredly, I say to you, I have not found such great faith, not even in Israel!"

The same consternation—and pity—was expressed for the scribes who wanted to argue theology when Jesus offered not only to heal but to forgive the paralytic lowered down before Him through the roof of a house where He was teaching. The leaders could not put themselves in the paralytic's place. They missed the miracle Jesus performed on the man's body and soul. But more than that—they missed the miracle needed in their own hearts. There was no poverty of spirit; no humility which could admit a need. There was only pride.

I've often wondered if the reason Jesus made so much of children and told people they had to become childlike to enter the kingdom of God was that a child can admit his or her need and ask for help. There's an inherent honesty that is too often lost in the mask of adequacy and pretense we call adulthood. We grow older but not wiser. Pride can make a prig or a prude, as well as a profligate!

The most subtle and serious form of spiritual pride is the desire to be adequate for God on our own. That was at the core of Israel's religious pride. No wonder Jesus congratulated those who were poor in spirit and could admit their need.

In my own experience, I have found that this very thing cuts me off from much of the grace God wants to give me. Often I try to deal with hurts and difficulties on my own strength so that I can offer the Lord a problem-free life. If happiness is the freedom to holler "Help," I miss a lot of the help available.

One of the most profound discoveries I have made in recent years has come through this first Beatitude. It has helped me learn that Christ comes to me down the corridors of my hurts and disappointments. He seeks entry to my heart not in my successes and victories alone. The deepest encounters I have had with our Lord recently have been when I have felt the helplessness of being poor in spirit and have dared to admit my need for God. By assuming that I have to pull myself together before going to Him, I cut Him out of a great portion of my life. Until I grappled with the deeper meaning of this first Beatitude, I had never seen this as pride.

Now, for me, humility is confessing my need immediately and allowing the Lord to heal me. I have never had a problem acknowledging that He was the source of any talents or gifts I may have. It has not been difficult for me to believe and say that all I am or have accomplished was the result of the Lord's incredible punctuality in providing strength and wisdom way beyond my abilities. But my problem is that I often hang on to aching problems, thinking that if I loved the Lord more or were more spiritual, I wouldn't have the feelings, resentments, or heartaches I sometimes endure. The thing I missed was the gift of crises to discover my own inadequacy and the Lord's sublime sufficiency.

And yet, here is the Lord Himself saying, "Congratulations, when you admit how much you need Me." It was a special word to an achiever like me. "You don't have to be an achiever to be loved," He seemed to say; "you are loved already. Now let Me help you where you hurt." Then this poor man ". . . cried, and the Lord heard him and saved him out of all his troubles."

I meet people with my brand of pride everywhere. Like the Laodiceans in Revelation, they say, "I am rich, have become wealthy, and have need of nothing." And the Lord says, "Do you not know that you are wretched, miserable, poor and naked?" The spiritual lukewarmness of the Laodicean church was caused by excluding the Lord from their deepest spiritual needs. As Wesley wrote to Francis Asbury, "O beware! Do not seek to be something! Let me be nothing, and Christ be all in all." The secret of that is to face honestly the knowledge that we desperately need the Lord in those hidden recesses of our hearts. It's strange: the greatest Christians of history were those who discovered that the closer they got to Christ, the greater their need of Him.

Recently, I visited the ruins of Philippi in northern Greece. At the excavated jail where Paul and Silas had been imprisoned, I sat alone, recapturing the time when the two adventurers sang psalms until the earthquake of the Lord's intervention set them free at midnight. I sang all the hymns I knew and then sang my way through the psalms, some of which I was sure they had sung. On the wall is a plaque with the words of Paul's confession, "For me to live is Christ" (Phil. 1:21). It occurred to me that that affirmation is more than a statement of purpose. It is a strategy for survival. For me to live abundantly, I need Christ. And I need Him in those areas where I often think I should be able to handle life on my own, rather than to depend on Him. An alternative wording of Paul's admission could be, "Christ is the source of life, way beyond what I could accomplish for Him on my own strength."

So often I am like Peter at the footwashing in the Upper Room: it's difficult to receive. But when I realize what I miss because of pride, I join with Peter in saying, "Wash all of me! I need you, Lord. Reach down into my inner heart and heal those things I have kept from you."

Now, look at the result of admitting our need. The happiness and power of the kingdom of heaven become available to those who express true humility. The kingdom of heaven means the reign, rule, and resources of God. When we surrender our lives to Christ and accept Him as Lord and Savior, we become citizens of His kingdom, now and forever. But it is as we acknowledge our need for Him in our lives and relationships that we realize more and more of the power of His Spirit in our spirit. The kingdom is already ours, but humility enables us to enjoy the limitless strength and wisdom that is stored up for us. It is good news that we don't have to make it alone; the grand assurance is that we will never face a need that is too big for the Lord. Now I know what the Psalmist meant, "Happy the people to whom such blessings fall! Happy the people whose God is the Lord!" (Ps. 144:15).

Last summer, I was part of a team of leaders conducting the Layman's Conference of Lake Junaluska. The speaker before me was spectacular. I overheard a conferee say, "I feel sorry for Lloyd, having to follow a speaker like that!" A twinge of competitive pride competed with the praise I felt for the way my friend had been used. I tried to put the competing spur out of my mind. When it came time to speak, I wanted to do my best but also needed the inner assurance that I had achieved. God blessed in spite of the distraction of human comparisons. Instead of pretending I did not have the tension of competition, I opened the corridor to allow the Lord to reach me. "I need You, Lord, to do what You want me to do. You know how achievement-oriented I become. Help me!" And He did. He blessed me and the people who listened. I had allowed Him to ask me the painful question, "Lloyd, who will get the glory?" And that's what happened. He got the glory.

Afterward, a long line of people formed to have me pray for the healing of their needs. I was exhausted from the long speech, but exhilarated by the number of people who could honestly ask for the Lord's help. The line seemed endless and the needs gigantic. At the end of the line was a man who shared an aching need in his son. I did not have the answers, nor the strength, for a long midnight conversation. I took his hands and told him we needed to pray for his son's healing. Inside I prayed silently. "Lord, help me!" Then I began to pray audibly for the young man. As I prayed, suddenly I felt someone grasp me on the shoulder. The grip was so strong I stopped my prayer to look around to see who was interrupting my prayer. There was no one there! The platform behind me was completely empty. And yet, Someone was there. The Lord. And the words of the Beatitude sounded in my soul. "Blessed are you, happiness is yours, for out of poverty of spirit you admitted your need. Enter the joy of My kingdom which is already yours."

THREE
WORDS
SPELL
HAPPINESS

"Blessed are those who mourn,
For they shall be comforted."
MATTHEW 5:4

It's a perplexing paradox! There's no way to avoid it. "Blessed are those who mourn, for they shall be comforted." What did Jesus mean by that? How can it ever be blessed, truly happy, to mourn?

Late one afternoon, as I sat in the beautiful garden on the Mount of Beatitude, overlooking the Sea of Galilee, studying Jesus' secret of true happiness, I had an experience which made the deeper implications of this second Beatitude come alive with freshness and power. Most of the day had been spent wrestling in prayer over the seemingly contradictory words *blessed, mourn* and *comforted.*

33

Then suddenly I was aware that someone else was there in the garden. I don't know how long she had been there. The woman was obviously distressed as she walked about restlessly. Her face was drawn and tired; the lines of strain and tension had made crevices of age beyond her years. She looked as if she both needed and wanted to cry but could not dare to allow her anguish to surface.

I returned to my studies, praying that if the Lord had her need on His agenda for me that I was ready and willing to help.

Later, she walked by my makeshift study desk. I smiled and said, "Hello." Her cautious response was in a lilting Irish brogue. I learned she was from Belfast, northern Ireland. She was the head of pediatric nursing in a hospital which cares for many of the victims of bombing and sniping incidents in that troubled city.

I encouraged her to sit down and talk. She eyed my Bible and books and inquired what I was studying so intently. I told her that I was searching for Jesus' secret of true happiness, spoken there on the mount so long ago.

"Happinesss?" she exclaimed. "That's one thing I doubt I will ever know again." The remark ushered us into a deep conversation about her life. She had come to Israel to rest and regain her courage. The suffering of the children in her ward had completely drained her. Her story about their mangled bodies and fractured psyches made me ache with her. We talked at length about her hatred of the I.R.A., her confusion about the complex issues of the unrest in her country, and, most of all, her bone-tired weariness.

When the time was right, I asked her why she felt she could not be happy again. I had a feeling there was something more, implied more in her sorrowful eyes than in her account about her patients.

She nodded agreement as tears finally began to roll down her tortured face. A long silence followed before she haltingly told me the reason for her self-imposed sentence never to be happy again.

One day as she was walking down the corridor of her hospital, she was called in to help turn a critical patient in a bed in the adult male ward. The doctor told her that the patient had massive fractures in his spine and neck from bullet wounds. Turning him on his side was absolutely necessary, but extremely dangerous. The nurse was assigned to turn his head as the doctor and male attendants turned his heavy body. One false or wrong move of the head, the doctor cautioned, would mean the man's life.

The Irish nurse's hands were shaking as she gestured and continued telling me the story. "I put my hands cautiously around the patient's head and then looked into his pain-ridden face. The man was none other than one of the leaders of the I.R.A. underground who was responsible for the suffering of the children I care for every day! I've never felt such hatred. With one move I could have killed him. And for a moment I wanted to! No one would have blamed me. It could have been an accident. Easily explained, but never justified. Finally, the nurse in me overcame my burning anger, and I turned the man's head with skilled caution and care. When we were finished, I walked out of the ward, down the hall, and out of the hospital, determined never to go back. I realized that all that hatred had gotten to me. That's why I had to get away. Now you know why I'll never be free to be happy again. When I realize what I almost did, or even that the thought could press through my mind, how could God forgive me? I'm no better than all the rest on both sides of the conflict. The cancer of hatred is eating me alive!"

The woman was mourning in grief over the whole mess. And in pity for the children, remorse over what she was capable of considering, soul-sickness over what was happening in her beloved country.

Deep inside me I heard the Lord say, "Blessed are those who mourn, for they shall be comforted. I have blessed this woman by helping her to get in touch with her anguish so that I can heal her. Tell her that I love her, that she belongs to Me, that she is a beloved person of Mine. She must allow Me to comfort her with My forgiveness. Then she must forgive herself. When she does that, she will be able to forgive the people she hates and be able to go back to work. All she needs to say in her mourning is, 'Lord, forgive me!' and 'I forgive myself!' Then she will be free to say, 'Lord, forgive them!' and finally with deep identification, she will be liberated to say, 'Lord, forgive us!'"

I told the woman what the Lord seemed to put on my heart to tell her. We talked about the promise of true happiness for those who mourn, and about the comfort of the Lord's forgiving power. After a long time of grappling with what I said, she seemed ready to pray. Though she had been raised a Presbyterian, she never had made a commitment of her life to Christ. She believed in Him, had prayed often for the children in the ward, and by some strange magnetic force had been drawn there to His land to find sanity and peace. But she had never accepted Him as Lord of her life. I told her about the Cross and His atoning death for her forgiveness. Then I led her through these prayers, each containing three words: "Lord, forgive me. I forgive myself. I forgive them. Lord, forgive us."

None of them was easy for her to pray, but each was said with authentic honesty and Celtic integrity. Anger had whittled away at her soul for a long time, and it was not a simple thing to dare to love again. Only the Lord's indwelling power could do that. The Holy Spirit, the Comforter, would be with her. She could be sure of that!

When we finished praying, she looked up and smiled for the first time in the hour and a half we had been talking. Her face was happy. Then she laughed. "I don't even know your name and what you do. You're not a Roman Catholic priest, are you?" she asked, catching herself in an old prejudice.

"No," I replied, "just a Presbyterian Christian from Hollywood." The woman left the garden, and I resumed my work.

"That's it!" I said to myself. To mourn means more than grief over the death of a loved one. The Greek word used to express Jesus' Aramaic word in the Beatitude is *penthein*, the strongest word in Greek for sorrow—the sorrow that pierces and breaks a person's heart; that is expressed in a person's face and reflected in his or her bearing. If being poor in spirit means the humility of recognizing and admitting our need, then mourning in the profound sense Jesus intended is the kind that brings us to confession and forgiveness of our sins. Again we ask: How can that deep kind of mourning bring happiness? Simply because it brings us to the three words that spell happiness: "Lord, forgive me!" The Christian life begins with these three words, and it grows with their constant repetition.

The Gospel is both bad news and good news. We

cannot accept the good news until we hear the bad news. The bad news according to Paul in Romans 3:23 is, "All have sinned and fall short of the glory of God." Sin is separation from the Lord or anything which keeps us from Him. The good news follows triumphantly in verse 24: "Being justified freely by His grace through the redemption that is in Jesus Christ." Those who can mourn over the separation from God are those who can experience the good news of His unmerited and unchanging love. Mourning over our essential condition of sin—running our own lives, being our own God, and determining our own destiny in arrogant self-will—is an absolutely necessary prerequisite to becoming a Christian.

Happiness is knowing the Lord. But we cannot meet Him as our Savior until we admit we are sinners: that's how the adventure of the new life begins. It's tragic to try to grow in a life we've never begun. And it all begins with the first time we say, "Lord, forgive me!" and accept the gracious forgiveness Christ lived and died to provide.

But that's only the first step. Look again at Paul's word to Timothy (1 Tim. 1:12–16). The Apostle goes back over the experience of mourning that brought him to Christ. He recounts that he was "formerly a blasphemer, a persecutor, and an insolent man; but I obtained mercy because I did it ignorantly in unbelief" (v. 13). It was on the Damascus road that he was struck down blind. In the three days that he sat in darkness, he was forced to experience something he'd never known before in his arrogant, achievement-oriented life: helplessness. Two things were undeniable to Paul: Christ was alive and he, Paul, was helpless.

The essence of spiritual mourning is the realization of what we have done with life and of our desperate need for the forgiveness of the Lord. Paul was comforted by the presence and power of the Lord because he was forced to get in touch with the man he was, and he longed to be forgiven. The comfort he received is explained in verse 14: "And the grace of our Lord was exceedingly abundant, with faith and love which are in Christ Jesus." He received faith to trust his life to Christ completely and to accept forgiveness.

The happiness we see in Paul all through his ministry came about because of the love relationship between him and Christ. Mourning had brought him to the three words that spell happiness. He accepted the bad news about his condition and experienced the good news of Christ's love. Paul's conviction and subsequent feeling of happiness are expressed in the summary of his theology in verse 15, "This is a faithful saying and worthy of all acceptance, that Christ Jesus came into the world to save sinners. . . ."

But that was only the beginning. The mourning that initiated Paul into the new life became the secret of intensifying the daily happiness of the abundant life. We didn't finish verse 15—purposely, so we could catch the full impact of the last words in the verse as the dynamic for staying alive in Christ: ". . . of whom I am the chief." Long after his conversion, Paul called himself the chief of sinners. The closer he came to Christ, the more he realized his need of Him. The Apostle never stopped mourning over areas of his life which needed to be changed. Mourning in this deeper sense keeps us moving spiritually, closer and closer to the full realization of the love the Lord has for us and is ready to give us each time we admit our need.

Note the difference between the two sons in Jesus'

parable of the prodigal. The lost son who mourned his separation from his father returned home and experienced forgiveness and reconciliation. He was able to say the three words which brought sublime happiness: "Father, forgive me!" The elder son who never left home, but was never really at home, could not mourn for his brother's plight nor rejoice with his return home. He was further from his father in spirit than his brother had been in the far country. He took his father and his generous inheritance for granted.

At the end of the account of the banquet at Simon the Pharisee's house (Luke 7:36–50), Jesus gives us the key: "He who is forgiven much, loves much." The woman of the street who anointed Jesus' feet out of gratitude for her forgiveness received the benediction "Go in peace." Not Simon. He had nothing to confess—or so he thought. He had measured his stature by his own specifications.

The realization of our smallness in comparison to the greatness of Christ and the stature He intends for us is cause for mourning and the prayer to be forgiven. Sin is the determination to remain small—in our thinking, in our evaluation of our potential, and in equalizing judgments of others to cut them down to our size.

We cannot escape the mystery of the abundant life. It is a constant rediscovery of the unlimited grace of our Lord and a persistent realization of what we do to limit it. We are never free of either. Both are necessary for growth: assurance and aspiration, confidence and confession. Boldness that there is nothing we can do to make our Lord stop loving us enables the bliss of admitting our failures.

In what areas of your life and mine do we need say, "Lord, forgive me!"? What are they for you? I know what they are for me. I mourn over those areas where I hang onto my own control and self-will. What makes you uneasy and uncomfortable in the Lord's presence? What keeps us from time in prayer with Him? What attitudes block Him? What habits keep us imprisoned? Where are we resisting the inflow of His Spirit? It is when we get a fresh vision of what life was intended to be that we mourn over what we've allowed our lives to become.

The experience is ever evolving as we grow in Christ. Nothing keeps us locked on dead center more than our unwillingness to forgive ourselves. Now the pronouns of the three words that spell happiness are: "I forgive myself." Refusal to forgive ourselves denies us the happiness of the blessed. Our lack of self-forgiveness is really our resistance to move on to new steps in Christ's strategy for us. Obsession with past failure is the surest way to avoid the challenge of experiencing the fullness of personal wholeness. Happiness is forgiving ourselves.

But the second pronoun of the three words that spell happiness must shift once again. Now the words spoken to others are: "I forgive you." The authentic test that we have accepted the forgiveness of our Lord is that we become forgiving people.

That's not easy. We ask with Peter, "Lord, how often shall my brother sin against me, and I forgive him? Up to seven times?" No wonder the big fisherman was astonished at Jesus' answer. He said, "I do not say to you, up to seven times, but up to seventy times seven." While the reluctant disciple was multiplying, Jesus taught a parable that went way beyond his limits of qualified love.

A king wanted to settle accounts with his servants. One owed him ten thousand talents—a million dollars in our money. When he could not pay, the king forgave the debt. Amazing generosity! We would expect the debtor to show in response an immense generosity to the people who owed him. But his reaction was just the opposite. When a fellow servant who owed him a hundred denarii (twenty dollars) could not pay, he had him thrown into prison. The plot intensified when the king learned of the forgiven servant's unwillingness to forgive. His words were biting: "Should you not also have had compassion on your fellow servant, just as I have had pity on you?" Now the tables were reversed and the ten-thousand-talent debtor who would not be to others what the king had been to him was thrown into prison. Jesus closed the parable with disturbing words: "So My heavenly Father also will do to you if *each of you*, from his heart, does not forgive his brother his trespasses."

According to Jesus, we can receive only what we are willing to give away. We cannot pray, "Lord, forgive me!" if we resist saying to others, "I forgive you!"

Let's take a relational inventory. Who in our lives needs our forgiveness? From whom do we need to receive forgiveness? Paul gives us the charter for the way we are to live: "Be kind to one another, tenderhearted, forgiving one another, just as God in Christ also has forgiven you" (Eph. 4:32). Happiness is saying we're sorry. Often we incarcerate a person in his or her feelings of remorse by not allowing him or her to talk out inner feelings of failure.

An African proverb puts it succinctly: "He who forgives ends the quarrel." But if we do not create the atmosphere in which a person can say, "I am sorry," we limit the depth of the future relationship. Let's not be too quick to say, "No need to say it. It was my fault as much as yours." We need to give a person time to talk out what he or she feels he or she did or said that hurt us. The best way to create a climate of graciousness is to be ready to ask forgiveness ourselves when we fail. A person who admits his mistakes becomes a person to whom others can readily say, "I am sorry!"

Giving and receiving forgiveness is really an expression of self-worth. We believe in ourselves as persons of value so much that we do not want to load our emotional systems with the virus of resentment. It's so much healthier to forgive and seek forgiveness. Anger, hatred, and resentment are life's most expensive emotions. They debilitate our spirits, tax our nervous systems, weaken our hearts, and confuse our minds. Eventually, unexpressed anger becomes the taproot of anxiety. It's turned in on ourselves.

A physician examined his patient thoroughly. All the tests were completed. He sat down at his desk to write out a prescription. The patient expected a powerful medication to cure his ills. All the doctor wrote was: "Your future happiness is dependent on being forgiven and forgiving!"

The last three-word combination which spells happiness is "Lord, forgive us!" As for the Irish nurse, there comes for us a time of creative acceptance of our part in the massive sufferings, wrongs, and injustices of our time. The Lord has called us to be people who mourn with Him over His creation.

When we allow ourselves to feel the needs of people, the segregation in our corporate heart, the toleration of unrighteousness, we no longer wring our hands and smack our lips in consternation. We say, "Lord, I'm part of it! I cannot expect of my city or nation any more than I do of myself."

The same is true of the institutional church. A very exciting thing happens to traditional Christians when they give up the luxury of criticism and do two things: become the kind of church member they want others to be; and accept the responsibility for the irrelevant ineptness the church so often models to the world.

There's a slogan that's very popular these days: "Are you a part of the problem or part of the solution?" The question is apt, but be sure of this: we cannot be part of the solution until we see ourselves as part of the problem. That too is a part of mourning.

I don't know about you, but Jesus' second Beatitude has given me no small measure of disquiet. Some basic questions need to be answered by all of us.

1. Have I ever admitted that my basic condition is sin? That I am separated from God? Have I ever made a start in the Christian life by saying, "Lord, forgive me!"—not for sins but for sin?
2. Am I able to ask the Lord to forgive whatever it is that separates aspects of my life from Him? On a daily basis? The Christian life begins with mourning over and confession of sin. It grows in dynamic power as we confess our sins. The closer we come to our Lord, the more we say, "Lord, forgive me!"
3. Have I ever said to myself, "I forgive me!"? It's the only way to turn from the past and move on in the adventure of new growth.
4. Am I able to ask for and freely give forgiveness? From whom do I need forgiveness? To whom do I need to give it?
5. Can I say, "Lord, I'm part of the whole mess our time of history flounders in today. Lord, forgive us!"?

If we can say yes to these five questions, we are ready to experience the comfort of God. The Greek word for "comfort" in the second Beatitude is inexhaustible in the richness of its meaning. Basic, and most important, is that it is the word that describes the companionship of the Lord with us. He is the Comforter who comes to us in our time of need. He is waiting, longing to invade us with forgiveness and love.

But the Comforter does more than accept and assure us. The same Greek word also means a helper who stands by our side—a witness, a counselor. He becomes our ally in life's battles.

Another exciting use of the word in Greek is for one who cheers another on in conflict, for example, a soldier's armor bearer. The Lord does that when we open ourselves with the three words that spell happiness.

The root word also means exhortation and encouragement. The Lord breaks open new areas for our growth and then gives us the strength to dare to move on.

The Holy Spirit, the Lord with us—presence and power—is the Comforter. All that He is ready to do in us and through us comes as a result of His anointing and infilling. Lasting happiness is not only knowing the Lord but being filled with His Spirit. That's the secret Jesus does not want us to miss in this Beatitude: we will be comforted—but only as we allow ourselves to mourn. And then, at whatever point we find ourselves with God, ourselves, others, or society, we can say the appropriate three words that open us to receive the comfort of His presence.

Well, there we have them: the three words that spell happiness. There is no lasting happiness until we experience and express forgiveness in the basic relationships of life. With God, we say, "Father, forgive me!" To ourselves we say, "I forgive myself!" With others, our prayer "Father forgive them!" becomes "I forgive you!" and then we stand with the suffering of our world and say, "Father, forgive us!" That's what it means to mourn creatively. Happy are those who express the need for forgiveness, for they will know the power of the Comforter!

THE DOOR TO HAPPINESS HAS TWO KEYS

"Blessed are the gentle,
For they shall inherit the earth."
MATTHEW 5:5

A few years ago, while traveling in the Highlands of Scotland, I stayed overnight in an ancient clan castle. The old laird of the castle was a jolly, kilted man with bony knees. He was as proud of the illustrious history of his clan as he was of his own distinguished military career in the Highland Guards. It didn't take much to prime an endless flow of talk about both all through dinner and late into the night.

Two things seemed to qualify me for a special kind of friendship. The laird reminded me that the Ogilvie clan had fought on the same side with his in many of the battles between the clans in Highland history. And he had good feelings about a "Dominie" visiting his castle. He called me "Padre," an affectionate term of esteem used by British soldiers for their chaplains. When he learned of my love of Scottish history, he treated me like a long-lost war buddy.

At the end of one of his stories, he leaned across the dinner table. His eyes twinkled under his heavy eyebrows; his voice lilted with laughter. "Padre, would you like to see my happiness room?" he asked with excitement. He explained that he kept the memorabilia of his clan's history in an old banquet hall of the castle. The ancient weaponry and clan history would interest me, he was sure, but I was really more intrigued with the fascinating name he had given his room! A happiness room—I wanted to see that!

As we walked down the stone corridor to the banquet hall, he told me how much he enjoyed spending time in the room where he could relive the great moments of his family's history. I noticed that he carried two large metal rings with an oversized key on each.

When we reached the gigantic, thick wood door of the banquet hall, I discovered the reason for the two keys. There were two locks on the door! The Scotsman gave me a knowing look when he carefully unlocked both locks. "The door to my happiness room is double-locked," he said with a confidential air. "It takes two keys to get to my treasures!" He seemed to enjoy the obvious parable he had given me. "Stick that in your sermonic cranium. I'm sure you'll make good use of that illustration in a sermon some day," he said.

I smiled in appreciation, tucking the insight into the sermonic file of my mind. It was there waiting for me when I grappled with Jesus' third Beatitude, "Blessed are the gentle, for they shall inherit the earth."

The door to true happiness is double-locked. It takes two keys to open, and Jesus gives us both keys in this powerful Beatitude. The blessedness of the truly happy is waiting behind a mysterious double-locked door of our human experience. The two keys are in the two words *gentle* and *inherit*. One key is relinquishment and the other receptivity: surrender and expectation, trust and hope.

A necessary prelude to understanding and living the mystery of authentic happiness locked in each of the Beatitudes is not only mining the riches in the meaning of the words but in identifying the human need each was spoken to heal. The Master's observation of the problems of people in the multitude, which also were sharply focused in His disciples, motivated the message of each Beatitude. What was it that His x-ray discernment identified in people and prompted Him to promise true happiness to the gentle who were adventuresome enough to claim their inheritance?

I think it was private enemy number one: tension! We all feel it at times. Some are never free of it. It's the mammoth, locked door of anxiety, uncertainty, and strain that has kept people from being happy in every age. When we get in touch with our tension, we can experience the prescription this third Beatitude gives us.

In the scientific world, tension is the act of stretching, the stress put on any material by pulling. And all metals have what scientists call the fatigue limit. If the tension persists, there will be a break.

In the psychological-spiritual realm, tension is mental and emotional strain caused by the pulling pressures of life. It's being pulled in different directions by conflicting demands and responsibilities. People. Their needs and expectations. Obligations, schedules and deadlines. We become uptight. Tense.

It takes two opposing, pulling polarities to stretch a wire taut to the point of tension. This is equally so for us as persons. We become the wire. Our mental capacity, emotional strength, and physical endurance become the metal which is stretched to the point of tension.

But who's pulling? On one side are the challenges and problems of life. On the other side—none other than ourselves! We pull back in desperate attempts at self-preservation. Many of the things we have to do are done under the duress of obligation or necessity. Another pull is fear. We are worried about our capacity or ability to do the things life demands of us. Or we pull in frustration over having to do things or go places we don't want. Tension is the result of the pull of our outer world against the desires and wishes of our inner world.

We feel tension not just when there is too much to do, but when we have to do what contradicts our wishes or values. Tension is the product of the conflict between our inner agenda and life's demands. Tension grows when we feel inadequate and must keep up a front of sufficiency. Or when we have thoughts and feelings we dare tell no one. Or when hidden guilts over the past demand immense energy to keep them covered. Or when some clandestine behavior must be concealed at all costs. The price is usually exorbitantly high.

We all live with tension and create tension. Most all tension comes from people. Their demands and desires often conflict with ours. Or they want us to do, be, or become something we resist or abhor. Tension can exist in a marriage when desires and preconceptions collide. We are pulled in a direction we don't want to go. It can grow between friends when criticism and judgments pull a person to please by contradicting his or her own self-worth. Tension grows in our work when we are pulled into a task which we are unwilling or unable to do.

An overloaded schedule is often blamed as a cause of tension. Not so! The real problem is deeper. Our schedules are a reflection of our choices. When we feel pushed and pulled by too much to do, it is because of our inner insecurity which has said "yes!" to more than we can do in the time we have. It is our resistance to life that is the culprit. Many people can do immense amounts of work and keep a heavy schedule with delight. The reason is that they enjoy what they are doing and want to do it.

An athlete can perform under great pressure without tension if he or she feels adequate and enjoys the challenge. Any entertainer can "get up" for a perfor mance and exceed natural talent if she or he is not against herself or himself and the audience. A writer under the pressure of a deadline can write inspired manuscripts if he wants to and has fun doing it. The great leaders of history performed under excruciating pressure without debilitating tension. Arnold Toynbee in *A Study of History* said that unrelenting pressure of necessity stirs the creative powers of people and brings out the greatness that is in them. The challenge, adventure, and excitement of being at the vortex of history's great moments spurs them on free of tension.

Horizontal tension pulls us apart. But vertical tension pulls us together. That's the secret of true happiness in the third Beatitude. Happiness is being pulled to creative tautness and into the very presence of God. And the two parts of the creative pull are gentleness and inheriting the earth.

You are probably saying to yourself, "What has gentleness got to do with tension? Inherit the earth? You only get what you fight for in life and that causes tension every day of our lives!"

The misunderstanding of gentleness in our usage is showing. We need to get back to the Hebrew word Jesus used and the Greek word translating it. Some versions of the Bible use *meek*. "How can the meek inherit the earth? They get chewed up by it!" we say.

The Hebrew word for gentle or meek is *anaw*. Jesus' Beatitude has its roots in Psalm 37:11. "But the meek shall possess the land, and delight themselves in abundant prosperity." The word *meek* is used to describe a person who, out of love and obedience, openly accepts the providence and guidance of God. He lives with the certainty of God's power and presence in all of life. The meek man or woman trusts that God knows what is best and will bring good out of evil. Gentleness really is surrender to God. In this magnificent Psalm, we are given nine imperative admonitions which express the essence of *anaw*.

1. Fret not yourself because of the wicked, verse 1.
2. Trust in the Lord, and do good; so you will dwell in the land and enjoy security, verse 3.
3. Take delight in the Lord, and He will give you the desires of your heart, verse 4.
4. Commit your way to the Lord; trust in Him, and He will act, verse 5.
5. Be still before the Lord, and wait patiently for Him, verse 7.

6. Refrain from anger, and forsake wrath! Fret not yourself; it tends only to evil, verse 8.
7. Depart from evil and do good; so shall you abide forever, verse 27.
8. Wait for the Lord, and keep His way, and He will exalt you to possess the land, verse 34.
9. Mark the blameless man, and behold the upright; for there is prosperity for the man of peace, verse 37.

Note the progression. The meek, or gentle, person does not take his or her measurements of life's success from the wicked, those whose lives are in habitual rebellion against God. Rather, the gentle person puts his trust in the Lord and seeks to know the good and do it. He is delighted by the surprises of God's intervention and provision. Gentleness is commitment of all our ways and worry to God, knowing He will act. The inner sign of gentleness is profound quietness that waits on God. The outer manifestation is freedom from destructive anger and debilitating wrath. There is an evident liberty in the gentle person. Most of all, he or she abides in the Lord and His Spirit abides in him or her. Surely, this is what Jesus meant when He said that the truly happy people are the gentle.

The Greek word to translate Jesus' Aramaic has a fascinating usage in Greek. It was used for an animal which had been tamed and brought under the control of the bit and reins, or an animal which had learned to follow the commands of its master.

In classical Greek, the same word was used for the mean between extremes. The meek or gentle person never went off in excessive directions but was distinguished by self-control that really resulted from the controlling power of a greater wisdom. Gentleness is neither recklessness nor cowardice, neither brashness nor lack of boldness. It is the perfectly timed, appropriately expressed, consistently reliable quality of those who do not go off in all directions, but are under the guiding control of truth.

Jesus' use of *gentle* in this third Beatitude is autobiographical. It was one of the qualities of His life that He specifically told His followers to emulate. The meaning of the Beatitude is to be discovered in His promise, "Take My yoke upon you and learn from Me, for I am gentle and lowly in heart, and you will find rest for your souls. For My yoke is easy and My burden is light." The whole incarnate life of the Son of God reveals the meaning of gentleness. He was completely open and receptive to the Spirit of God. Obedience was the essence of His life. "Not My will, but Thine be done!" was His constant prayer. Christ is gentle meekness for us to behold.

The yoke of Christ is the lesson from which we learn gentleness to replace our tension. The Lord offers us an exchange of yokes. Instead of the yoke of tension, He offers the liberating yoke of obedience which results in gentleness. When we are yoked to Christ, we come under His control, guidance, and pacing. In ancient times, a training yoke was used to train a young animal. The heavy end of the yoke was carried by an older beast who had to take the weight and responsibility of the burden. All the trainee had to do was keep pace, go in the same direction, and not pull off in one way or the other. Now we see how gentleness is learned by being yoked to Christ. We surrender the control of our lives and all our affairs to Him. Gentleness really means unreserved commitment to Him.

Paul discovered the secret of how to experience and emulate gentleness. He describes it as one of the fruits of the Spirit. That's it! Gentleness is possible only as Christ lives His life in us. The fruit of the Spirit is a description of the character of Christ. But it takes a total relinquishment to have the gentleness of Christ pervade our nature. That, too, is His gift. The Spirit breaks our pride and softens our aggressive willfulness. Then we can surrender all our needs, hopes, and dreams to the Lord.

Now we can understand why gentleness in this profound sense is one key to the double-locked door to happiness. Tension is the result of pulling away from the Lord and His plan and purpose for us. Our circumstances, other people, and the demands of life are not the cause of our tensions. The cause is being out of control because we are under our control rather than the Lord's.

Let's get in touch with whomever or whatever is making us tense. We cannot catch a ball with a clenched fist. Nor can we receive the Spirit of God with a clutched heart.

Have you ever surrendered that specific person or problem to our Lord? Are you willing to do that right now? Then are you willing to wait for what He will do? Many of us are at the fatigue limit right now because we are unwilling to trust the Lord. Solomon gave us the secret: "Trust in the Lord with all your heart, and do not rely on your own insight. In all your ways acknowledge him, and he will make straight your paths" (Prov. 3:5–6, RSV).

When I identify the people and situations in my own life which cause tension, I realize that I am trying to live in those relationships and responsibilities on my own strength. God is invading those areas right now. Will I let go of my control and accept His control? My happiness in this moment depends upon my relinquishment.

The same is true for a businessman with whom I had lunch the other day. He's a tightly wound spring, a grim, anxious man. Creativity and happiness elude him. His belief in Christ as Savior has not reached the liberating point of accepting His lordship over the pressures which are pulling him apart. In conversation, we took the pressures one by one and surrendered them to our Lord. There's enough time in every day to do the Lord's will by His power!

A woman with tension written on her face and expressed in her body language came to see me. She was dependent on sleeping pills to rest and pep pills to make it through the day. Aggression was expressed in the way she attacked all her obligations and responsibilities. "How do you learn to relax?" she asked urgently. "I'm a Christian, but it doesn't seem to help me in my daily living. I've become both hard and harsh with the people around me. What am I going to do?"

I told her she had to come apart or fall apart. Each day she would have to take time apart from her tension-filled life to condition her mind with the love and power of our Lord. Each day she would have to surrender that day's responsibilities and pressures to the Lord. She would have to give up playing God over her life. That was the basic sin, and the cause of tension.

But that's only one key to the double-locked door. The other is found in the words *inherit the earth*. The word *inherit* in the Scriptures means to claim a possession promised by God. The children of Israel were promised the land of Palestine as an inheritance. Then the Lord promised them the kingdom fulfilled in the glory of the

Davidic kingdom. Later in Israel's history, the promise turned toward the expected reign of the Messiah.

The phrase *inherit the earth* for Jesus meant more than territory upon the earth, but a quality of life lived on earth. All that Christ has accomplished through His life, death, resurrection, and imminent presence is our inheritance. "All things are yours," said Paul.

Indeed! We are "joint heirs with Christ!" Nothing that we either want or need is left out. Claiming the inheritance of our forgiveness, redemption, and Christ-filled lives frees us to live expectantly. An inheritance is residual. Its resources are applied to life's challenges and problems. Our inheritance is not only what Christ did but what He will do in those situations which cause tension in us. We can relax only if we know that the Lord will act at the right time and in the ultimately creative way.

The gentle can wait for each new payment of their inheritance. They have been called to reign with Christ! He told those who trusted in Him that they would inherit the kingdom prepared for them (Matt. 25:34), and the gift of eternal life (Matt. 19:29), in quality now and forever. What more do we need? The kingdom of God is His reign, and eternal life is the intimate relationship with God which begins now and which death cannot end.

Paul speaks of the "glorious inheritance of the saints" (Eph. 1:18), and Peter reminds us that in Christ we have "an inheritance incorruptible and undefiled, and that does not fade away, reserved in heaven for you." But note that Peter goes on to tell us that daily payments of that inheritance are given to the gentle, "who are kept by the power of God. . . ." (1 Pet. 1:4).

The power of God, the Holy Spirit, is our inheritance to be received in life's tensions. The legacy of the Lord was,

"You shall receive power when the Holy Spirit has come upon you" (Acts 1:8). That's the inexhaustible inheritance we can depend on. We will never be left alone. Sufficient power will be given for each demanding tension. The gifts of the Spirit are ours—wisdom, knowledge, discernment, insight, and faith. We will have all that we need for each situation. Life is unpredictable, but the Lord's presence will be predictable.

What the Holy Spirit will give in us will be coupled with what He will do around us to surprise us. Expectancy and true happiness are inseparable.

The Lord's question to us is the same as the Scottish laird's, "Would you like to see my happiness room?" Our inheritance is there waiting. But the door is double-locked. Here are the keys: the surrender of gentleness and the expectation of our legacy. And our response is to take the keys and open the door.

THE HAPPINESS OF A CONSUMING PASSION

*"Blessed are those who hunger and thirst for righteousness,
For they shall be filled."*

MATTHEW 5:6

Know how you feel when you're on the edge of making an important discovery? Like there's something brewing in your mind and you know you are near a crucial breakthrough? An excitement grips you as you become convinced that there is something more, something deeper, than you've known or experienced before. It's the driving enthusiasm of a scientist who knows he or she is near discovering the cure for a dreaded disease. Or the intensity of an inventor as she or he gets closer to finding a secret never before utilized. Or the urgency of any of us as we sense that we're about to find the answer to a seemingly impossible problem.

I've had that feeling all through my preparation to write this chapter. My life is people and their needs. You. I think of you when I study and as I write. The problems and potentials we all share are my constant concern as I seek to penetrate the depth of the incredible resources of God's love and power in Jesus Christ. It's the search for ways to unlock the meaning and the might of the Bible to help us maximize life that spurs me on day by day. And then, there are special times like that I am experiencing now, when I am convinced that there is an untapped power available in a particular verse that's never been found before. All the research is done, the original Greek and Hebrew checked and all the commentaries and expositors available read, out I still feel the Spirit pressing me on to a deeper discovery, a more incisive insight, an explosive idea.

I haven't been able to shake the excitement of a fresh discovery as I've thought and prayed about what Jesus really meant when He said, "Blessed are those who hunger and thirst for righteousness, for they shall be filled." The one thing that kept me pressing deeper was the exclamatory and congratulatory usage of the word *blessed:* "O the happiness of" or "Congratulations, you favored ones!" or "True happiness to you beloved who belong to the Lord!" Then I noted that the congratulations were not being given to those who had arrived at righteousness, but those who hungered and thirsted for it. It must have shocked the disciples to hear their master congratulating them for their hunger and thirst. How unlike the Pharisees who thought they had righteousness and ruthlessly admonished others to attain it by thousands of rules and regulations! There's not the slightest note of "ought" in the Lord's tone or intention. The parent in me always slips it in and says, "You ought to be poor in spirit, mournful, gentle, merciful, and then God will bless you." Not Jesus!

All these thoughts were spinning around in my mind when I went to bed one night this past week. My final prayer before falling asleep was, "Lord, I feel you have something more You want to reveal in this Beatitude. Please help me see it, live it, share it, with people I love!"

Then, just before I awoke, I had a dream. I was standing in front of thousands of people. The Lord drew near and stood beside me.

"What's the greatest need in these people?" He asked, "and what's the one thing you want to ask Me to give them?"

My response was immediate. "Salvation . . . so they can live forever."

"No, Lloyd," He said, "they already have that. I completed that two thousand years ago. It's theirs!"

"Forgiveness, then, Lord?" I suggested.

"Not that, either," He said.

"Well, then," I said, thinking about our present search for authentic happiness, "that they will experience true happiness rooted in grace and joy, and expressed in daily living?"

"You're getting closer, but you've missed the target. Press on!" the Lord retorted.

"Surely, then, the gift You want to give is Your presence and power!" I said, feeling that at last I had hit it.

"No, there is something more than that. My presence is already impinging on their consciousness, ready to release My power. The gift I want to give is the one that makes all you've suggested possible. There's no salvation, forgiveness, happiness, or power without it."

"Tell me, Lord!" I pleaded.

"I want My people to want Me!" he said winsomely and tenderly. "I long for My people to long for Me as much as I long for them."

"But, Lord," I protested, "I thought that the desire to know You was our gift to You, not Your gift to us. Isn't that what we do to claim what You've done for us?"

"That's where you have missed it! You and so many generations. You want to take credit in choosing Me. You think it's some kind of human accomplishment when you think through truth and decide you can believe. Or when you give up the human struggle with problems and perplexities and decide to trust Me. Or when you make a mess of things and need My forgiveness. These are not your gift or achievement, but My grace.

"Allow me to sear into your mind a basic, liberating truth: *what I desire, I inspire.* The longing to know Me and have a right relationship with Me is My primary gift to My people whom I have chosen to belong to Me. The hunger and thirst of a consuming passion for Me is not a human choice but My blessing. I have made you right with Me through the Cross. You *are* forgiven. Even the desire to express your righteousness in all relationships and responsibilities is My gift. There is nothing you can do to be righteous. You are already. The gift of faith follows the gift of divinely inspired discontent. But remember even that gift comes from Me. Happiness is being a willing receiver!"

When I awoke, the dream was still vivid. All that I had been studying and mulling over had been invaded by an insight, a revelation, which radically changed the direction of my interpretation of the fourth Beatitude. All the blessed characteristics of the happy people enumerated in the Beatitudes are not humanly induced qualities but imputed gifts from our Lord. What He desires from us,

He inspires in us. My thinking and understanding suddenly gelled. This Beatitude is a congratulatory recognition by our Lord of people who had already received the gift of a consuming passion.

So, if you long to find God, congratulations! He's already found you. If you urgently desire to know Him, it's because He has created the desire within you. If you are not right with Him and want whatever it is that is separating you to be forgiven and healed, it's because He's at work in your soul. If your heart burns with a consuming passion to know and do His will in all of life, that blaze has been set by the flame of God!

G. K. Chesterton caught the sublime blessing of a burning passion.

> In a time of sceptic moods and cynic rusts,
> And fatted lives that of their sweetness tire,
> In a world of flying loves and fading lusts,
> It is something to be sure of a desire.[1]

To be sure of a desire! Are you sure what you want? Is it the Lord? If so, He willed you to want what He wants to give: Himself and a completely right relationship with Him.

T. S. Eliot in "Little Gidding" puts it this way,

> All shall be well
> All manner of things shall be well
> By the purification of the motive
> In the ground of our beseeching.[2]

---

[1]Quoted in James S. Stewart, *King For Ever* (Nashville: Abingdon, 1975), p. 63.

[2]From "Little Gidding" in *Four Quartets* by T. S. Eliot, copyright 1943 by T. S. Eliot; copyright 1971, by Esme Valerie Eliot; reprinted by permission of Harcourt Brace Jovanovich, Inc.

What's at the ground of your beseeching? Has the Lord touched you with a divine discontent? If so, you are very fortunate, because the answer is on the way. He is purifying the motive and the content of your beseeching.

Luke's account of this alarming Beatitude is much briefer and even more pointed. It puts the emphasis on the consuming passion. "Blessed are you who *hunger now*" (6:21). It was Matthew who remembered the righteousness for which we are to hunger and thirst. Luke alone has the warnings, the "woes" which drive home the point of each Beatitude. "Woe to you who are full *now*, for you shall hunger" (v. 25). Jesus ached over people who had no passion to know God and be right with Him. He looked lovingly after the rich young ruler who didn't want the kingdom of God more than anything in all the world. And He wept over Jerusalem because the Holy City, His beloved people, did not either know or want the things which belonged to their peace . . . nor the time of their visitation . . . by the Messiah.

It's alarming to note that Jesus condemned those who were satisfied with their relationship with God and commended those who hungered and thirsted for God. Remember the parable of the children at play: "To what shall I liken the men of this generation, and what are they like? They are like children sitting in the marketplace and calling to one another, saying: 'We played the flute for you, and you did not dance; we mourned for you, and you did not weep'" (Matt. 11:16–17). We can picture two groups of children taunting each other with shouts over the marketplace. One group wanted to play weddings and the other funerals. They couldn't get together to play either, because they didn't know what they wanted. The parable sharply delineated those who didn't like John the

Baptist because he was austere from those who criticized Jesus because He was too affirming of life. The result was that they didn't know what they wanted. Most of all, they didn't really want God. Except on their terms.

Wherever Jesus went, he commended the earnestness of those who wanted God and His power for their needs: the centurion who pressed through the crowd begging Jesus to come heal his son; the Samaritan woman who persisted in seeking the healing of her daughter. Or think of the pertinacity of the woman who followed Jesus in the teeming crowd until she succeeded in touching His garment. The parables of the importunate widow (Luke 18:1–8) and the neighbor at midnight (Luke 11:5–8) call for earnestness. The Lord affirmed a consuming passion. He knew that those who expressed the earnestness of it had been given the gift of holy desire.

When Christ affirmed the God hungry and thirsty, He based His Beatitude on rich Old Testament Scripture. I wonder if He had Psalm 42:1–2 in mind: "As a hart longs for flowing streams, so longs my soul for thee, O God" (RSV) or Psalm 63:1, "O God, thou art my God, I seek thee, as in a dry and weary land where no water is . . ." (RSV). The Lord had been through the temptation of the wilderness not long before He gave the Sermon on the Mount. The conviction that "man shall not live by bread alone, but by every word that proceeds out of the mouth of God," from Deuteronomy 8:3, sustained Him. He knew from fresh experience that the hunger for the Word of God was itself a gift of God. Amos's quote of God may have been remembered. "Behold the days are coming," says the Lord God, "when I will send a famine on the land; not a famine of bread, nor thirst for water, but of hearing the words of the Lord" (Amos 8:11, RSV). And

Jesus knew He was the bread of life and water for those who thirst. He was the end of the famine! That's why He gave accolades to the hungry and thirsty. They acknowledged the emptiness He had come to fill. The Spirit of God had given them a gift of appetite and thirst.

I remember calling on a woman in the hospital whose sickness had diminished her appetite and thirst. I'll never forget the happiness she expressed when she was taken off intravenous feeding and began to feel thirst and hunger pangs again. "I never knew what a blessing it was to be hungry," she said.

The same is true for spiritual hunger and thirst. It's a miracle of God when He breaks through our diminished appetite that has been sated by distracting satisfactions which have left us undernourished and dehydrated spiritually.

A man said to me recently, "I'm really very dissatisfied with my life."

"Congratulations!" I exclaimed.

"What do you mean by that? Didn't you hear me? My life is a mess. I'm not happy at all about the way things are going."

My second exclamation didn't please him any more than my first. "You are very fortunate!" I said.

I went on to explain. "Thank God for your dissatisfaction. He's got something much better in store for you. The discontent you feel is a sign that you are a special, chosen person. The Lord is invading your life!"

As we talked, the man became very excited about what the Lord may be saying to him. But more than any change in his life, the real longing was for an intimate companionship with God.

So often, the things we find wrong in ourselves, other

people, or our situations are manifestations of our yearning for God. He wants us to experience His love for us. Then we can see what's wrong in a different perspective and how they might be made right by His guidance and power. It never works to try to set things right until we are right with God. We only make a worse mess of things . . . and leave a trail of human wreckage along the way.

I talked to a woman who was filled with negativism and criticism. What's worse, she felt the boomerang of self-condemnation for having the feelings she had. I encouraged her to cry it all out. Then I said, "There's a deeper need in you, isn't there? You're really very dissatisfied with yourself. Thank God for that. He's trying to reach you. Why don't you let Him love you? Your discontent is the Lord's way of showing you that you need Him. For yourself, first, and then as the source of strength to become a creative person to positively right the wrongs you are distressed about."

The essence of Jesus' blessing in this Beatitude is what the Lord said to the people of Israel while in the Babylonian exile: "Then you will call upon me and come and pray to me, and I will hear you. You will seek me and find me; when you seek me with all your heart" (Jer. 29:12–13, RSV). God wants us to seek Him with a consuming passion. But the desire to seek Him comes from the promise which precedes the admonition: "I know the plans I have for you, says the Lord, plans for welfare and not for evil, to give you a future and a hope" (v. 11). He's always beforehand with us. Our seeking is the result of having been sought. He offers us a new future and a hope. We come hungry and thirsty to know not only the plans but the Author of the plans—God.

The Lord's instigation is clearly promised in His own

words, "Before they call I will answer, while they are yet speaking I will hear" (Isa. 65:24, RSV). In the fifty-fifth chapter of Isaiah, the same assurance is given. Everyone who thirsts is to come. No longer will bread alone satisfy. "Seek the Lord while he may be found, call upon him while he is near; let the wicked forsake his way, and the unrighteous man his thoughts; let him return to the Lord, that he may have mercy on him. And to our God, for he will abundantly pardon" (vv. 6–7, RSV). It is because the Lord is near that we want to come to Him. We want to come to Him because He has come to us with mercy and abundant pardon.

The consuming passion of the blessed, the truly happy, is for righteousness. What God wants us to want is freely offered. Righteousness is a right relationship with God. And He creates in us a longing for that just as a starving person desires food and a parched person craves water.

The Greek used to translate Jesus' words in this Beatitude employs the accusative rather than the genitive case. When the genitive is used to express a desire for an object, it means a desire for part of the object; the accusative, however, implies the desire for the total object. It is for the totality of righteousness that we are given the gift of hunger and thirst.

That means four things. First, the word *righteousness* is used in Scripture to describe God's essential nature of absolute purity, truth, justice, and love. Our consuming passion for righteousness is for God Himself, for companionship with Him—an intimate oneness.

The second meaning of righteousness trips us. It means knowing and doing the will of God in all of life. He gave us the commandments as the delineation of righteousness. When we measure our lives by the righteous standard of God, we are engulfed with frustration and failure. We can't even get past the first. In fact, that's the reason all the rest are so difficult. We want to be right on our own, justified by our own goodness, loved because we have measured up. Self-righteousness! Perfectionism leads to pride, our inadequacies to self-condemnation. A grasping desire for righteousness on our own strength to please God leads to anything but happiness. We still feel the alienation because of what we've been and done.

That leads to the good news of the third use of righteousness. The righteous God came Himself to establish righteousness with us. When we could not come to Him, He came to us. Jesus Christ was called the Son of righteousness. Apt description! He took on Himself the sin of the world and died on the Cross as a final sacrifice for our unrighteousness. The good news is that in Him we are made righteous with God. The only way to understand the promise of this Beatitude is to accept the free gift of forgiveness and reconciliation He established for us. The righteous judgment of God has been satisfied once and for all. He has made us right with Himself! Now and forever.

That's what gripped Paul and turned his life around. He had tried to please God on his own. He had relied on self-justification. But then the Lord invaded the bastion of his blatant blasphemy of trying to be righteous on his own strength. He was loved and forgiven, reconciled and released. The consuming passion of his life became righteousness. Listen to him: "For I am not ashamed of the gospel of Christ, for it is the power of God to salvation for everyone who believes. . . . For in it the righteousness of God is revealed from faith to faith; as it is written, *'The just shall live by faith'*" (Rom. 1:16–17).

It is by faith that we accept for ourselves the righteousness we have through Christ. But even that faith is a gift.
The same righteous God who came in Christ to make us
right with Himself comes to us in His Holy Spirit to give
us the gift of faith. Again, what He desires, He inspires.
Faith is not an accomplishment; it is the primary gift of
the Holy Spirit. The Lord first creates in us a desire for
Him, gives us a hunger and thirst for being right with
Him, reveals the gospel of righteousness through Christ
and the Cross, and gives us the power of faith to believe.
That enflamed Paul's passion. "For by grace you have
been saved through faith, and not of yourselves; it is a gift
of God, not by works, lest anyone should boast" (Eph.
2:8–9).

The more sure we become of our righteous status
through Christ, the more He becomes our passion.

That brings us to the fourth use of righteousness. When
we know we are right with God by faith, we have a
creative motivation to be faithful and obedient in all of our
relationships. We now feel a consuming passion to be
right and reconciled with others. People and their needs
become our passion. Any person who does not know the
Lord's love and any area of injustice in our society become
part of the Lord's agenda for us. But here again, He goes
before us. He puts on our hearts any broken relationships
which need healing. He gives us marching orders to get
involved in situations of human need. Insight, discernment, courage, and love are provided. Interpersonal and
social righteousness are something He engenders in us.
And we are freed to spend ourselves, not to become
righteous but because we are already! And all of this is
because we are called and chosen to be the elected people
of God. That's what Jesus is affirming in the Beatitude.

It's what Paul knew for himself and wanted the Christians at Rome to claim. The word is for us: "And we know that all things work together for good to those who love God, to those who are the called according to His purpose. For whom He foreknew, He also predestined to be conformed to the image of His Son, that He might be the firstborn among many brethren. Moreover whom He predestined, these He also called; whom He called, these He also justified [made righteous]; and whom He justified, these He also glorified" (Rom. 8:28–30). And that means you and me!

One final thing the Lord seemed to be saying to me as I wrote this: we can be sure we have caught the true happiness Jesus affirms in this Beatitude if we could go one step further. If the Lord congratulates us for having received the gift of a consuming passion, we are now free to thank God and congratulate ourselves. Dare to say, "Blessed am I indeed! I have been elected, called, chosen, cherished, and beloved, for I know that more than anything else in all the world, I want the Lord. It's His amazing gift to me. I am right with Him by the faith He empowered in me. Now I want to do right because I am righteous through His love and forgiveness." Praise God. What He desires, He inspires!

HAPPINESS
IS
YOUR PAIN
IN MY HEART

"Blessed are the merciful,
For they shall obtain mercy."
MATTHEW 5:7

If you had to choose one word to describe the nature of God, what word would you choose? All-powerful? All-knowing? Forgiving? Gracious?

My word would be *merciful*. Whatever other words I might use are all part of this magnificent quality of mercy. I'm not alone in my choice. In the Old Testament alone, the word is used nearly two hundred times to describe the nature of God. The Hebrew word, *chesedh*, means both identification and empathy, involvement and intense feeling. It describes the feeling of getting inside a person's skin and feeling what he or she is feeling, hoping, or aching. God knows and cares about what's going on inside us. Mercy is our pain in His heart!

79

We need to savor that. God is not up there or out there, aloof from our needs. The mercy of God, from my experience and the biblical witness, is His favor, forgiveness, forbearance, and fortuitous intervention. Our pain in His heart results in outgoing, ingoing, and ongoing love for each of us. The Psalmist summarized all the aspects of mercy when he exclaimed, "Bless the Lord, O my soul; and all that is within me, bless his holy name! Bless the Lord, O my soul, and forget not all his benefits, who forgives all your iniquity, who heals all your diseases, who redeems your life from the Pit, who crowns you with steadfast love and mercy, who satisfies you with good as long as you live so that your youth is renewed like the eagle's" (Ps. 103:1–5, RSV).

That's our theme song! Everything within us wants to bless the Lord because He can feel our pain in His heart and respond with unmerited favor for us, forgiveness even before we ask, forbearing our rebellion and sin, surprising us with fortuitous, on-time blessings when we expect them or deserve them the least. The experience of the mercy of God is the basis of trust and confidence, strength and courage, hope and joy.

But why is it so few feel the happiness of the mercy of God? The Psalmist goes on in Psalm 103 to tell us. "But the steadfast love of the Lord is from everlasting to everlasting upon those who fear him, and his righteousness to children's children, to those who keep his covenant and remember to do his commandments" (vv. 17–18, RSV). Ah, there it is. A true experience of mercy results in awe, never taking God for granted. Those who receive mercy keep the covenant and do the commandments. The two great commandments were to love God and one's neighbor as oneself (Deut. 6:4–5; Lev. 19:18).

God's people were to be distinguished by having His nature imputed. The recipients of mercy were to be merciful. But were they? The sad account of the people of God is that they were not—neither to each other nor to other nations. The Old Testament closes with the pleas of the prophets for the people to do justice, have mercy, and walk humbly with their God. But not even their refusal took their pain out of God's heart; it only intensified it. That's why He came, mercy incarnate, in Jesus Christ. Favor indeed. Forgiveness unreserved. Forbearance unlimited. Fortification while we were helpless. A manger. A vivid personification of mercy. A cross. The resurrection. Merciful comfort in the Holy Spirit.

When Mercy Himself revealed the heart of God, He put it clearly so we could not miss it. "Blessed are the merciful, for they shall obtain mercy." A congratulatory challenge. "Bravo to the merciful!" He said. "You can experience more of the mercy of God!"

Let's be sure we understand what Jesus did not mean before we consider accepting the gift of what He did mean. This Beatitude does not imply an assurance that if we are merciful toward others that they will be merciful toward us. Our own experience, coupled with a review of history, affirms the fact that there's no guarantee of mercy from people to whom we've been merciful. Often, there is just the opposite. People are stingy receivers. The scales are seldom balanced.

Nor did Jesus suggest that we are to be merciful in order to assure God's mercy. There's no bartering with God. The Lord meant something deeper. There's a profound secret in this Beatitude. It tells us as much about ourselves as it does God.

Mercy is the one thing we can't give unless we've had

it. This is an essential truth. Mercy can't happen through us until it happens in our hearts. We can give away only what we are in the process of experiencing. So Jesus is saying, "O how blessed, truly happy, are the people who are experiencing mercy because they can be merciful, and as they are, they will be open to receive more!" If we lack mercy for others, the secret is not to try to be merciful but to allow God to give us a fresh experience of His steadfast love. The greatest gift we can give the people around us is to accept God's mercy for us. The result will splash out of our overflowing hearts onto the people we love or need to learn to love.

The ultimate test is that we feel other people's pain in our hearts. Mercy is my pain in God's heart. But when I realize that, I can enter into fellowship with Him in feeling your pain in my heart. And our expression of mercy has the same four elements in it as God's mercy to us. We will communicate affirming favor, forgiveness of people's failures and mistakes even before they ask, giving them the freedom to dare to ask. Forbearance expressed in patience and a million second chances will be communicated. And people will be amazed at the ways, in spite of everything, that we intervene to become involved in lifting their burdens, comforting their hurts, and sharing their pain. Mercy is getting inside people's skin, just as God got in ours when He came to live among us.

The Beatitude confronts the blockage in our spiritual plumbing. Our lack of mercy to others makes it impossible to receive the mercy God wants to give us. If we will not share His heart, we cannot experience the mercy of His heart.

The mercy of Jesus Christ knew no geographical or

national boundaries. It reached out in congratulations to a good Samaritan who felt the pain of a wounded traveler on the Jericho road who had been bypassed by merciless religionists. For Jesus, mercy was no longer reserved as the mandate of Hebrew for Hebrew. The abhorred Samaritans, Romans, and Greeks were included in His *chesedh*-filled heart. And His death on the cross was mercy for all people.

Most of us find it difficult to live in the shadow of that merciful cross in our judgments. We are constantly tempted to break the First Commandment. We put ourselves before God and decide whether or not a person is worthy of receiving our mercy. James nailed it down. "For judgment is without mercy to the one who has shown no mercy. Mercy triumphs over judgment" (James 2:13).

The other day a man told me he could not forgive what his wife had done to him. "Then I hope you never fail!" I said. The man was alarmed. Then I pressed him to tell me of the times in his life when he had felt the mercy of God. He found that difficult. No wonder he was so hard on his wife's failure. I tried to tell him about his pain in God's heart, the forgiveness that had been given before he asked, the continuing relationship as if he had never ever failed, acceptance in countless new beginnings. When I went back over Calvary and the immensity of God's mercy, the man's hard shell of judgmentalism was finally cracked. With a fresh realization of mercy, he was able to make a commitment to be merciful to his wife as God has been to him.

Some time after that visit, I talked to his wife. She was grateful for the breakthrough her husband had made. She said, "He said that he forgave me, but it's so difficult for him to change his attitude toward me. I keep feeling I must do something to measure up because of my mistake. It's hard to live with a merciless pout."

A merciless pout! So often we say we forgive or try to express in-spite-of love but hold another person at arm's length with our hurt and bruised feelings. We create a purgatory for people to wait in until we decide they are worthy of our acceptance.

Many of us think of ourselves as magnanimous people who express forbearance and forgiveness. But the favor is lacking. Our body language shouts our lack of mercy in a bland tolerance or a sticky sweetness that hides our real feelings.

Paul challenges us to show mercy with cheerfulness (Rom. 12:8). The word for "cheerfulness" in Greek is *hilarotees*, from *hilaros*, meaning "hilarity." Mercy with cheerful laughter and joy! There's an antidote for a merciless, purgatorial pout!

It's so difficult to give up our right to punish people. We feel we must balance the scales by our reserved feelings and attitudes. Eventually, the anger is turned in on ourselves, and we become anxious and depressed.

But remember that Paul called for hilarious mercy only after he had reminded his readers of the mercies of God. "I beseech you therefore, brethren, by the *mercies* of God, that you present your bodies a living sacrifice, holy, acceptable to God, which is your reasonable service. And do not be conformed to this world (and its lack of mercy!), but be transformed by the renewing of your mind (fresh experiences of God's mercy), that you may prove what is that good and acceptable and perfect will of God." On the basis of that, we can hear the challenge, given to the Christians at Rome, not to think of themselves more highly than they ought to think, "but to think soberly, as God has dealt to each one a measure of faith" (Rom. 12:1–3, parenthetical additions mine).

A sober evaluation of the mercies of God bursts forth in hilarious mercy. When we review how merciful God has been to us, we can't contain the flow of mercy through us. The inflow and outgo become one constant experience.

The same triumphant note is sounded at the end of chapter 3 and the beginning of chapter 4 of Second Corinthians. "But we all, with unveiled face, beholding as in a mirror the glory of the Lord, are being transformed into the same image from glory to glory, just as by the Spirit of the Lord. Therefore, seeing we have this ministry, as we have received mercy, we do not lose heart" (2 Cor. 3:18–4:1).

Paul thought of the mercy of God along with grace and peace in his letters to Timothy.

"Grace, mercy, and peace from God our Father and Jesus Christ our Lord" (1 Tim. 1:2). Grace is God's outgoing love; mercy is ingoing love, peace is the ongoing experience. Receiving and giving mercy maintain the flow of grace. Peace is the abiding sense of being accepted and loved.

Paul reminded the Ephesians that God is rich in mercy. And yet, for his own relationships he had to rediscover again and again what being merciful meant. The account of his relationship with Mark is a good example that even a spiritual giant like Paul had trouble being merciful to a young missionary failure who had defected in Pamphylia. The Apostle refused to take Mark along on a subsequent missionary journey at the cost of contention with Barnabas, and in fact, their parting. But near the end of Paul's life he wrote to the Colossians, commending Mark as one who is with him in prison, and affirms him with love. Fresh mercy had been received and expressed.

I wonder about the Marks in my life—and yours. Who needs mercy from us? The best way to experience the impact of Jesus' Beatitude is to take two sheets of paper, draw a line down the middle of each sheet, and on the top of one, write, "Experiences of God's mercy in my life." On one side of the sheet, list the specific occasions. On the other side, note the aspects of mercy which were realized by you in that incident. Favor? Forgiveness? Forbearance? Fortuitousness? That exercise will flood our hearts with gratitude.

Now take another sheet. On the top, write, "Relationships in which I want to communicate mercy." On the one side of the sheet, list the persons and situations specifically. Then on the other side, put down which of the four aspects of mercy most needs to be mediated through your words, attitudes, and actions. Describe what you will say, how you will look and act, as you express mercy.

Two things will happen. You will be amazed again that God has your pain in His heart. Suddenly, you will feel the pain of others in yours. No longer will there be negative judgment or aloof, uninvolved sympathy. Your heart will beat with the Lord's. And at the deepest levels of your soul, you'll hear Him say, "Congratulations, blessed one! You now know the true happiness of feeling what others are feeling. The mercy you have received from Me will now flow from you to them. You and I are one in the ministry of mercy!"

HAPPINESS
IS
HAVING EYES
IN YOUR HEART

7

"Blessed are the pure in heart,
For they shall see God."
MATTHEW 5:8

Think of the many different ways we use the words *I see*. We say, "I see," when we focus something with the vision of our eyes. What a magnificent gift seeing is! We can behold the wonder of God's signature in the natural world.

But we use the same words for intellectual comprehension. We say, "Oh, now I see!" when truth has been registered in the issues of our brain with understanding. After the gift of insight into some complicated thought problem, we say, "I never saw that before." A scientist in his laboratory, upon making a great discovery, will say, "Now I see what I've been searching for!"

89

In the same way, in the realm of spiritual growth, we say, "I now see myself as I am and see God in His love and forgiveness." Spiritual perception is seeing. We exclaim, "I was blind and now I see!" when we receive the gift of faith.

Also, in interpersonal relationships when our intuitive capacity is exercised with empathy, we express our identification with another person in mixed metaphor, "I see how you feel." With the gift of our hearts, we "see" with x-ray penetration into the emotional condition around us. We are able to see what is happening to us and others. We see with the gift of wisdom.

The reason for the multiple uses of the words *I see* is that we have eyes in our hearts as well as in our heads. In the sixth Beatitude, Jesus congratulates those who have 20/20 heart-eyes. "Happy are you! Congratulations to you! You are blessed, you who are single-hearted, for with your heart-eyes you shall see God." The Beatitude offers a potential and a promise, and, in between, a problem. It is an affirmation and an assurance, and the danger of an affliction. We all have eyes in our hearts, but not everyone sees.

Jesus did not single out some of those with Him on the Mount of Beatitude to tell them of their special endowment denied to others who listened. He spoke congratulations to the whole crowd. Jesus was a master communicator. He was not negative, saying, "What's the matter with you? You have eyes in your heart, but you haven't seen God!" Rather, He told all present that they had heart-eyes and would see God—when their hearts were pure.

The positive impact of that promise is impelling. Surely it made everyone want to know what a pure heart was. How effectively Jesus helps us to want what He wants to give us. He tells us of our power to see; then He leaves it up to us to evaluate what we've done with it.

Consider first, then, the amazing potential entrusted to us. The Scriptures are full of references to the vision of the eyes of our hearts. The Hebrew meaning of *heart* includes intellect, emotion, and will—the heart in the totality of our inner capacity to think, feel, and decide. The eyes of the heart, therefore, include comprehension, discernment, insight, wisdom, vision, and perception. With this God-given endowment, we can "see" what He is doing and saying and planning. In prayer we can be guided into truth. We can observe the wonder of God's handiwork in the world and what He wills for us in all of life. Our heart-eyes are given to us to see what He sees!

But with every potential there is the possibility of a problem. We can distort the finest gifts of God. That's why He came in the Messiah: to heal the eyes of our hearts. In rebellion against God, we lost our vision. Jesus quotes Isaiah 6:9–10 in His deep concern that our separation from God has impaired our capacity to see. "For the heart of this people has grown dull. Their ears are hard of hearing, and their eyes they have closed, lest they should see with their eyes, hear with their ears, should understand with their heart, and should turn, and I should heal them" (Matt. 13:15). We are sure those who listened to that were alarmed.

But then once again Jesus challenges with a compliment. He says to His followers, "But blessed are your eyes for they see, and your ears for they hear; for assuredly, I say to you that many prophets and righteous men have desired to see those things which you see, and have not seen them, and to hear those things which you hear, and have not heard them" (Matt. 13:16–17). Note the affirmation which prompts an honest evaluation of whether our eyes have been healed and whether we are using them to take in all Christ offers us in Himself and His kingdom. The freedom to accept Him as Messiah and Lord is a gift, as we clarified in our study of the fourth Beatitude. Peter's heart-eyes were healed when he could answer Jesus' question on the road to Caeserea Philippi with, "Thou art the Christ, the Son of the living God." The latent capacity of seeing Immanuel, God with us, had been invested in the heart-eyes of the disciple. But so few saw. Why?

The problem is lack of purity of heart. Lecturing on this Beatitude years ago, James Moffatt defined purity as single-mindedness. "Blessed are they who are not double-minded, for they shall be admitted into the intimate presence of God." Sören Kierkegaard said, "Purity of heart is to will one thing." The use of the word *pure* in the Old Testament is fascinating. It described liquids without admixtures, metals without alloys, an army without defectors, grain that has been winnowed, a person free of debt, and a sacrificial animal without blemish. The Psalmist asked, "Who shall ascend the hill of the Lord? And who shall stand in his holy place? He who has clean hands and a pure heart" (Ps. 24:3–4, RSV), and in a time of great contrition prayed, "Create in me a clean heart, O God, and put a new and right spirit within me" (Ps. 51:10, RSV). In both psalms the Hebrew for *pure* means undefiled, cleansed, without distortion, with singleness of motive. Isaiah used the word *pure* to mean clean from sin. Habakkuk tells us that God has pure eyes, and Jesus tells us that our heart-eyes, like God's, can be pure.

The secret of purity of heart is unveiled in Matthew 6:22–24. Jesus said, "The lamp of the body is the eye. If therefore your eye is good, your whole body will be full of light. But if your eye is bad, your whole body will be full of darkness. If therefore the light that is in you is darkness, how great is that darkness! No one can serve two masters; for either he will hate the one and love the other, or else he will hold to the one and despise the other." The Greek word translated "good" here in the New King James comes from *haplous,* meaning single. That helps us in our understanding of purity of heart. It is singleness of desire and purpose. William Barclay extends that insight in his translation of the Beatitude, not unlike Moffatt. "Blessed is the man whose motives are entirely unmixed, for that man shall see God."[1]

Single-mindedness is not simple-mindedness or narrow-mindedness. Rather it is the result of putting God first in our lives. An unreserved commitment enables a riveted attention.

Recently, I met a man who told me that he earned his living as an "attention getter." That caught my interest. "What do you mean?" I asked. His reply was fascinating. "My job is to get the attention of the American people. I am an advertising executive. It is my task to use everything I can—media, print, billboards—to impress the people with the absolute necessity of buying the products I promote."

That same week I met with a group of businessmen who talked about the one thing in their lives which made it difficult to be faithful and obedient to Christ. The last man to share cut to the core of our inability to see with our hearts. "I have too many commitments competing

---

[1]William Barclay, *Daily Study Bible* (Philadelphia: Westminster Press, 1977), vol. 1, *The Gospel of Matthew,* p. 101.

with my ultimate commitment. I'm going in a hundred directions. I think about the Lord only in a crisis." A distracted attention—the man's heart was not pure, single, focused. All he could see were the confusing demands.

A woman confessed the same problem in a different way. "What do you do with a wandering attention? When I pray, I can't keep my mind on God for more than a few minutes. I drift off into all sorts of worries, fears, and fantasies."

All these encounters occurred while I was thinking about our heart-eyes and why so few Christians see. James gives us more of an answer than we want. Speaking of the doubter, he says, "For let not that man suppose that he will receive anything from the Lord; he is a double-minded man, unstable in all his ways. . . . Purify your hearts, you double-minded" (James 1:7–8; 4:8). What is in our hearts determines what the eyes of our heart see. It is what's inside that counts. The old saying is wrong: "What you see is what you get." In the light of this Beatitude it should be, "What you've got is what you see." When we focus our attention on the Lord and open our hearts to Him, He comes within us to dilate our spiritual vision.

A man who had just had a cataract operation was amazed at what he could see again. He said something we all may need to say. "Now that I have had the cataracts of my eyes removed, I need your help to remove the cataracts of my soul. I feel a murky, cloudy, fuzzy veil over my heart." We talked at length about his longing to see with his heart. Though he was a church member, he had never committed his life to Christ nor invited Him to take up residence in him. He had no ultimate priority. His life had drifted among a multiplicity of loyalties and responsibilities. I explained Jesus' promise in this Beatitude and asked him if he wanted a pure, single heart in which Christ reigned supreme. He did and we prayed together.

That day in the hospital was the turning point. Some months later, he came to see me. "I'm amazed at what I can see of God in my own life and the world around me. My eyes in both my head and heart have been opened!" Paul would have been pleased. What he prayed for the Ephesians had happened to this man. I shared the verse with him and it is now his life verse. "I do not cease to give thanks for you, making mention of you in my prayers: that the God of our Lord Jesus Christ, the Father of glory, may give to you the spirit of wisdom and revelation in the knowledge of Him, the eyes of your understanding being enlightened; that you may know what is the hope of His calling, what are the riches of the glory of His inheritance in the saints" (Eph. 1:16–18). The same gift is offered to all of us. All we need is the desire of a Bartimaeus. When Jesus asked what he wanted Him to do for him, his response was clear, decisive, insistent: "Lord, I want to see!" The same petition is the prelude to the healing of the spiritual eyes of our hearts. And Jesus' word is, "You receive not because you ask not."

Tennyson's persistent prayer was for a "clearer vision of God." We all long to be able to say with a Jacob, "I have seen the Lord and my life is preserved," or with a Job, "I have heard of Thee with the hearing of the ear but now my eye sees Thee." That will require saying with William Cowper:

> The dearest idol I have known
> Whate'er that idol be,

Help me to tear it from Thy throne
And worship only Thee.

The vision of God is in Jesus Christ. He is God's
heart opened for us to see. What is God like? Let us
look to Jesus Christ! Give Him our total allegiance,
and we will be able to see. And when we do, we begin to
see what we have never beheld before. We will see
ourselves in our need of Him, others in their need of our
love, and the future with clear guidance. William Wordsworth said,

Heaven lies about us in our infancy!
Shades of the prison house begin to close
Upon the growing boy.[1]

A penetrating conversion reverses that astigmatism of
the heart. Then we can say with Robert Louis Stevenson,

Sing me the song of the lad that is gone,
Say, would that lad be I?
Give me again all that was there,
Give me the sun that shone!
Give me the eyes, give me the soul,
Give me the lad that's gone.[2]

And the Lord is more ready to answer that prayer than
we are to ask. In fact, the desire to pray it comes from
Him!

One of the most crucial aspects of having our heart-eyes

---

[1] *Ode: Intimations of Immortality*, v, in *Complete Poetical Works of William
Wordsworth* (New York: Houghton Mifflin Co., 1904), p. 354.
[2] *Songs of Travel*, xliv, in *Complete Poems of Robet Louis Stevenson* (New
York: Charles Scribner & Sons, 1905), p. 192.

healed is being able to see people through the lens of Christ's love. Like the man who had double healing, we will see more than men as trees walking; we will see people. With our new eyes of our hearts, we will be able to see beyond what people do to what they are. We will have the sublime combination of empathy and discernment.

A woman exclaimed wistfully, "How I wish my husband could see me. The real me! He looks at me but somehow he looks right past me. I try to tell him about me but he doesn't *see* what I'm saying." The tragedy is that her husband is Christian, but has never had Christ's healing touch on the scales over his heart-eyes. His wife and his friends all long for him to be healed. He is missing the wonder of intimacy in which the essential *I* meets the real *you*.

A personal word. I had been a Christian and a pastor for several years before I had an experience which healed my heart-eyes. It was when I discovered the promise of the indwelling Christ that I began to see. A new discernment came as a result. I began to see beneath the surface of people and events. The indwelling Lord refracted my spiritual vision and gave me x-ray intuition. I saw the meaning of the Scriptures as never before. An understanding of how to communicate Christ's strength for people's struggles was imputed as a gift. Sensitivity in situations multiplied my analytical capacity. Most of all, I began to "see" my family and friends. I could say with Elizabeth Barrett Browning: "Earth's crammed with heaven, and every common bush afire with God."[1] And

---

[1] *Aurora Leigh*, bk. vii.

the secret was in saying yes to the Lord's offer to live in me and be my heart eyes. Christ Himself is the eye of the heart.

Happiness is having eyes in your heart. Congratulations to the single-hearted, for you will know intimate communion with the Lord and see with His eyes!

THE FIRST STEPPERS

"Blessed are the peacemakers,
For they shall be called sons of God."
MATTHEW 5:9

There is a delightful New Year's Eve custom in Scotland called "first-footing it." The idea is to be the first person to step across a friend's threshold to wish him "Happy New Year!" and toast his health and happiness.

I want to build on that tradition in establishing what might be "The Holy Order of First-Steppers." Or it could be called "The Happy Fellowship of Initiative Reconcilers."

The only qualification necessary is that we be willing to take the first step. We all want to be first in something. This is our chance! We can be first-stepping peacemakers.

Our motto could be Jesus' challenging seventh Beatitude: "Blessed are the peacemakers, for they shall be called sons of God." The various translations of the Beatitude shed penetrating light on the meaning. The New English Version has it, "How blest are the peacemakers; God shall call them his sons." J. B. Phillips renders it, "Happy are those who make peace, for they will be known as the sons of God!" William Barclay's incisive translation is, "Blessed are those who produce right relationships in every sphere of life, for they are doing a God-like work."[1] My own study has resulted in something like this: "Happy are the initiative enablers of peace with God, themselves, and others, for they are the kin of God in the healing of the wounds of the world." However you put it, the impact of the Beatitude is the same. We are called to receive the peace of Christ and to take the initiative in sharing it in life's relationships and responsibilities.

The difficulty is in taking the first step. The old saying is true: the longest journey begins with the first step. It is not easy to go first in expressing forgiveness or seeking reconciliation. A woman said to me recently, "Why should I go to her? She hurt me! Let her take the first step." She missed the joy of being a first-stepper. A man confessed, "I'm filled with resentment and I'm depressed. I resent people, my job, and what life has dealt me." I tried to share that his inverted anger was causing the depression. We talked about the people he resented. "Why not go to them and talk out how you feel? Find out the causes of the broken relationships. Seek forgiveness

---

[1] *The Beatituaes and The Lord's Prayer for Everyman* (New York: Harper and Row, 1975), p. 100.

where you're wrong and give forgiveness where you've been wronged." His response excluded him from being a first-stepper. "Why should I do that? I'm the one they should come to." "Would you forgive them and make peace if they did?" He was not ready for that question or the cost of the answer.

None of us finds it easy to be an initiator in making peace. It is a demanding, soul-stretching responsibility our Lord has given us. We cannot do it without Him. He is the patron of the first-steppers, and patron means pattern and defender. What He guides, He provides!

Peace is a key word of Jesus' life and ministry. He came to establish it, His message explained it, His death purchased it, and His resurrected presence enables it. The messianic predictions were that He would be the Prince of Peace (Isa. 9:6). The angels who announced His birth sang, "On earth, peace, good will toward men!" (Luke 2:14). His persistent word of absolution to sinners was, "Go in peace!" Just before He was crucified, the Lord's last will and testament was, "Peace I leave with you, My peace I give to you; not as the world gives do I give to you. Let not your heart be troubled, neither let it be afraid" (John 14:27). When the Lord returned after the resurrection, His first word to the disciples was "Shalom." Peace. The life of Jesus was saturated with His mission to bring the peace of God and to initiate the healing relationships of peace with God.

The early church was the original chapter of the "Holy Order of First Steppers." They were distinguished by the peace they received, shared, and preached. "Preaching peace by Jesus Christ" is the testimony of their central calling in Acts 10:36.

Paul opened and closed his letters with the word *peace*

No wonder! It described his own profound experience and liberating conviction. "Therefore, having been justified by faith, we have peace with God through our Lord Jesus Christ" (Rom. 5:1). Bottom line of the Apostle's teaching is that the sure test that we have accepted the Lord's initiative love is that we know lasting peace. The Hebrew word *shalom* meant perfect welfare, serenity, fulfillment, freedom from trouble, and liberation from anything which hinders contentment. But it was not until Paul met Christ and was filled with Him that he discovered a peace which was completely unassailable by trouble. He found peace in trouble, not freedom from trouble.

A true first-stepper has discovered that peace with Christ ushers us into the peace of Christ. The enmity and strife are over. Separation and fear are gone. Christ, the original first-stepper, has stepped into our hearts with forgiveness and acceptance even when we did not deserve it.

Peace is a sure sign that Christ has taken up residence in us. From within, He assures us that nothing can make Him stop loving us. He has settled our destiny on the cross. Paul knew that and wrote, "For it pleased the Father that in Him all fullness should dwell, and by Him to reconcile all things to Himself, by Him, whether things on earth or things in heaven, having made peace through the blood of His cross" (Col. 1:19–20).

When we share that bold conviction, we can allow "the peace of God to rule in our hearts" (Col. 3:15). The word for "rule" in Greek is "umpire." He calls the shots and keeps us from anything which would rob us of the peace He died to give us. He guards our hearts with His peace. "Be anxious for nothing, but in everything by prayer and supplication, with thanksgiving, let your requests be made known to God, and the peace of God, which surpasses all understanding, will guard your hearts and minds through Christ Jesus" (Phil. 4:6–7). Peace will be protector and guide. It will settle our jangled nerves, and in the midst of conflict and confusion, give us the assurance that all will work together for good because the Lord is in charge. That's the gift we are given to become first-steppers.

But we cannot give what is not real to us. Peacemaking begins with an experience of peace in our own hearts. When we have received the gift of peace, we know an ordered and harmonious functioning unity, wholeness, a being knit together. That is what happens when the character implant of Christ in us takes place. The fruit of the Spirit is ours. "The fruit of the Spirit . . . is peace" (Gal. 5:22).

Our first step as peacemaker is toward ourselves. Most of us find it difficult to initiate peace with others because we are not at peace with the person who lives in our own skin. We need to meet that unique person inside. Often we are harder on that person than anyone else. We find it difficult to forgive ourselves, even after we've heard and accepted the forgiveness of the cross. But it is blasphemy to contradict the Lord, and He has loved us unreservedly. We need to ask Him to help us love ourselves as much as He does. That alone will free us of self-condemnation, negation, and lambasting. A test of our acceptance of ourselves as Christ-loved and forgiven persons will be abiding peace. A profound center of calm is the result of creative delight and enjoyment of ourselves. Happy are the peacemakers—with themselves.

The natural overflow of that inner peace will be a

transformed attitude toward the people around us. Then we can become initiating peacemakers with others. That first-stepping ministry has three parts: making peace between us and others; between people we know who are separated from one another because of misunderstanding, hurt and hatred; and between groups in our society. Paul gives us marching orders for all three: "Therefore, let us pursue the things which make for peace" (Rom. 14:19).

Think of the broken relationships of your life. With whom are you at odds? For whom do you continue to hold grudges or memories of hurts? Whom have you harmed or distressed whose forgiveness you need to seek? Take an incisive inventory. List the names and the memories. Happiness awaits action. A letter, a phone call, a visit—a first step. If we know of anything for which we need to say we are sorry and ask for forgiveness, this is the day. If we need to share our feelings with a person who has wronged us, make this a "Do it now!" day. Knowing what unresolved tensions do to our peace of mind and our health, it is an act of self-esteem and preservation not to wait. Do it for Christ . . . do it for yourself.

I find it crucial to talk to the Lord about what I've done or what people have done to me before I talk to them. It gives me perspective and tenderness. The Lord helps me see the deeper needs in the relationship and what has caused the problem. He also shows me myself and what I have done and said. His forgiveness provides a fresh experience of grace for my first-stepping reconciliation. He helps me imagine how to act and what to say. When I surrender the conflict to the Lord, the tension is released and I can accept my calling to be a channel of peace. A peacemaker does not "make" peace; that has already been done on the cross. Our calling is to appropriate and mediate the peace of Christ in the specific relationship that has been fractured by us or others.

The one thing we can say with certainty about our feelings is that they are ours. We may be wrong or confused, but we still feel strongly. Our task as first-stepping reconcilers is to express our feelings in a way that does not make others defensive. The best way to do that is to own our feelings and express our need to be honest about how we feel. Rather than attacking, our responsibility is to tell the other person simply and clearly about how what has happened has made us feel. Often our feelings can be transformed by talking and sharing graciously.

If we need that emotional cleansing, so do others. A first-stepper is sensitive and aware. With the Spirit's imputed empathy, we will be able to see and feel when a person has feelings which need to be shared. Love demands our initiative effort to provide an opportunity for communication and an ambience of acceptance. When people know that our love is unqualified and unconditional, they will be liberated to talk until they know they are understood. A peacemaker can quickly admit whatever he or she has done or said which has caused pain. When we are falsely accused, we can share that we can imagine how the person feels and then share the situation in question from our perspective. Reconciliation is more crucial than being right! When Christ is present, He leads people to a new beginning. The past can be forgotten. The miracle of healing will be His gift.

Now we need to consider our calling to be first-steppers where conflict exists between people. The peacemaker can hear both sides without taking sides. Loving is listening. Enabling questions help. Encouragement is expressed when we tell people we understand how they feel. That does not mean that we agree or that we add fuel to the fires of their angers or hostilities.

After we have heard both people, our next initiative is to encourage direct confrontation. Offer to arrange it and to be a moderator and mediator. Something like this needs to be said: "You have told me how you feel. It is not important that I agree or disagree. I appreciate how you are feeling. But now you need to talk directly to this person. You'll not be free until you do. Will you allow me to arrange a time? I'll be there if it will help. Don't put it off. You are too valuable to Christ to allow these feelings to fester. Love Him and yourself enough to deal with this broken relationship."

All this is dependent on our having earned the right to be reconcilers. That comes from deep trust and confidentiality. It is also nurtured by our openness about how Christ has helped us when we have known the pain of being misunderstood or misused. The sharing of our experiences will free the persons we are trying to help to deal with their feelings. We become fellow-sufferers rather than aloof arbitrators.

Prayer is the inner power of the peacemaker. The Lord wants reconciliation more than we do. He will show us each step of the healing. Prayer begins with Him. He calls us into conversation to give us the gifts of wisdom, discernment, and healing. Pray before, during, and after. One of the most effective ways to help people break through to new attitudes and willingness is to pray with them. Pray with each person involved in the conflict and then pray with both or all of them together. When people ask the Lord for reconciliation, the barriers begin to come down. Often little more than a prayer for the will to be willing is the beginning of healing.

Our ministry of reconciliation between groups is equally demanding. It requires that we be captured by neither group. Our challenge is to become the bridge over the troubled, turbulent waters which divide the groups. That means we must have credibility with both groups, without losing our integrity. Conflict is usually caused by power struggles. The unspoken question is "Who's in charge here?" It implies the desire to control. So many lofty theological battles and congregational schisms are simply battles for control. The peacemaker dares to ask both groups, "What is the real issue beneath the lofty rhetoric? What if we loved Christ with all our hearts, and wanted His peace more than victory? We cannot be separated from one another without eventually being separated from the Lord. What does His love demand?"

Groups are usually the reflection of strong leaders. Often the cause of conflict between groups is the bruised or slighted egos of these leaders. Our peacemaking will demand a combination of sensitivity and incisive honesty. There will be times of boldness when we must confront people with what they are doing to themselves and others. When division persists, eventually we must "speak the truth in love." And we are never alone. The indwelling power of the Lord who is our peace will guide us. Not only will He lead us each step of the way, He will also be at work in those we are trying to help. When we least expect it, He will change the impossible situation. Trust Him!

A vital credential of a peacemaker is freedom from

gossip. Nothing disqualifies us in being reconcilers more than talking *about* people rather than talking *to* them. The old Spanish proverb is on target: "Whoever gossips to you will gossip of you." Relationships are strained and guarded when we are not absolutely trustable. When we gossip about others, always the question can linger of what we will say about them. A peacemaker never says anything about another person that he has not first said to that person directly. After that, why tell anyone else?

The reward of a peacemaker is to be called a son of God. There is no greater joy for parents than to have their children want to be like them. God has made us sons and daughters to reproduce His character in us. The last part of the Beatitude gives us the secret source of our strength to be peacemakers. God is an initiator. He came in Christ. He loves us before we respond, forgives us before we ask to be forgiven, blesses us even when we are undeserving. And when we accept our status as His cherished, beloved children, we begin to grow in His likeness. We shall be like Him in spreading peace. Paul shared this same secret with the Corinthians. "Become complete. Be of good comfort, be of one mind, live in peace; and the God of love and peace will be with you" (2 Cor. 13:11). In other words, if we want to know God, we must join Him in what He is doing.

Jesus called for action. Obedience is the key that unlocks the resources of His Spirit. "If you know these things, happy are you if you do them" (John 13:17). Hearing and doing are inseparable.

William James underlined the crucial relationship between hearing and action. He reminded us that no matter how full a reservoir of truths we may possess and however good our sentiments may be, if we have not taken advantage of every concrete opportunity to act, our character will remain entirely unaffected. "A character is a completely fashioned will," says James. It is a compilation of tendencies to act in a specific and decisive way. These tendencies become permanently ingrained in proportion to the frequency in which we follow through with action. When a resolve or an opportunity is neglected or refused without action, it works to hinder our future capacity to implement what we believe. Our growth in our sonship is dependent on being first-steppers in the adventure of peacemaking. To delay it or neglect it today will make it more difficult tomorrow. Why not now?

The other day on a flight across the country, I had an amazing conversation with a man seated next to me. I was busy collecting and writing down my thoughts on this seventh Beatitude. Out of the corner of my eye, I noticed his interest in what I was doing. Finally he interrupted, asking what I was working on so intently. "I'm writing the charter for a new organization," I replied playfully. "A what?" he exclaimed. "What is it called?" I smiled and said, "The Holy Order of First-Steppers!" That started a long conversation about initiative peacemaking. I shared much of what I have written in this chapter. "That's not easy," he said. We talked about the difficulties of being a reconciler. The thing he returned to repeatedly was the idea of expressing and seeking forgiveness. I knew a raw nerve had been touched in him.

When the plane landed in Chicago, he prepared to get off. "Where to now?" I asked. "Home . . . to be a first-stepper," he replied. He went on to tell me about a tragic breakdown of communication with his wife. Few words and no affection had been given for months. He told me that he had been determined not to be the first to resolve the tension because he had felt his wife was wrong. Now he knew it was his move; he was responsible to take the first step.

We shook hands. "Power to you, first-stepper!" I said. "And to you!" he replied with new joy.

A
DARING
FRIENDSHIP

*"Blessed are those who are persecuted for righteousness' sake,
For theirs is the kingdom of heaven."*

MATTHEW 5:10

I want you to meet my best friend. I've known him for thirty-two years. He's been with me through trials and tragedies, pain and persecution, ups and downs, success and failure. He is the kind of friend who knows all about me and never goes away. He has a special way of helping me to see myself and do something about it. He accepts me the way I am, and yet that very acceptance makes me want to be all that I was meant to be in spite of all the difficulties around me. He laughs with me over my mistakes and weeps with me in my sorrows. He has been faithful all through life's battles. I have never been left alone when I suffered criticism, hostility or resistance for doing what love demanded. He is with me when truth triumphs and is always there to absorb the anguish of defeat in a righteous cause. We share a vision, a hope, a dream together . . . my friend and I. As a matter of fact, he gives me the daring to be true to what I believe regardless of cost. He meets all the qualifications of a real friend: he loves without limit; he is loyal when others turn away; he listens to my hurts; and he liberates me to grasp life with gusto, regardless of the consequences. I have only one hope: when I come to the end of this portion of heaven and pass on to the next, the one thing people will remember is that I was his friend. My best friend is Jesus Christ!

Does that sound presumptuous? Are some of you wondering if I have slipped from my intellectual objectivity and drifted into sloppy subjectivism? Is there possibly a twinge of arrogance expressed in my bold assurance? Before you answer, check the Bible. Can friendship be used as a sublime expression of our relationship to Christ? Yes, at His invitation! "No longer do I call you servants, for a servant does not know what his master is doing; but I have called you friends, for all things that I have heard from My Father I have made known to you. You have not chosen Me, but I have chosen you and appointed you that you should go and bear fruit, and that your fruit should remain, that whatever you ask the Father in My name, He may give you" (John 15:15–16).

It is in the context of this abiding friendship that we can dare to grapple with the frightening and awesome challenge of the eighth Beatitude. Once again, we stagger under the impact of the paradox. "Blessed are those who are persecuted for righteousness' sake, for theirs is the kingdom of heaven." Happiness in persecution? How can that be? Trials, difficulties, suffering? We all have them. How can we be happy in them? We can't—unless we face them with Christ as our friend. And His faithful word of friendship is, "Lo, I am with you always."

The word *friend*, when used for the Savior, Messiah, and Lord of all creation, must express more than the best of human examples of friendship around which we define what it means to be a friend. Rather, it is from Christ that all human friendships are judged. We know what it means to be a friend to others when we have an intimate companionship with the Lord.

That friendship is absolutely necessary to understand and live the implications of this Beatitude. In fellowship with Christ, we discern what we are to say and do as an expression of our love and loyalty to Him. When that guidance leads us into just causes and sacrificial obedience, we can be sure He will be with us. So often we get into trouble for the wrong reason. Our own personality quirks, insensitivity, or ego needs get us involved in tight places the Lord has not guided us. Persecution for righteousness' sake is something very different. It is joining the Lord in what He's doing in the battle against Satan and his legions of evil people and insidious institutions.

The kingdom of heaven promised us in the Beatitude is not a reward but a present reality. It is best defined as friendship with the King of that kingdom. Our life with Him defines the marching orders of our daily life, which may result in persecution. He alone can give us the courage to say, with Luther, "Here I stand; I can do no other." But before the reformer said that, he had discovered a union with Christ and a righteousness through faith alone. The remarkable, daring leadership he gave was with his Leader before him to show the way, behind him to encourage him, above him to watch over him, beside him to give courage, and within him to give supernatural power to endure persecution and rejection. The blessed happiness Christ promised those who were persecuted was none other than His friendship through it all.

When Christ spoke this awesome Beatitude, He knew what was ahead. He had done battle with Satan in the wilderness. He realized what would happen when he confronted the establishment and organized religion. In His soul, He knew rejection, betrayal, suffering, and the cross were ahead. He also foresaw what would happen to His beloved followers. And for the worst that would happen, He offered citizenship in the kingdom of heaven. Two realities would never be separated—conflict and the comfort of His companionship. We can take anything with that assurance.

Friendship with the King of the kingdom gives us both charter and courage. The terms *kingdom of heaven* and *kingdom of God* are used interchangeably. They both imply, as we have mentioned earlier, the reign and rule of the Lord in all of life. Because we have been made right with God through faith, we can now live boldly in extending the kingdom—not to earn our righteousness, but because we have been made righteous through Christ. When that assurance pervades our minds, hearts, and wills, then we can pray for guidance about our next steps in extending the kingdom into every relationship and responsibility of our personal lives and every structure and institution of our society.

The more profound our friendship with Christ, the

more urgent we will be in our kingdom ministry. We move from "I want" to "Lord, what do You want?" to "I will!" And when difficulties result and hardships come, we can be sure of the Lord's intervention. Lincoln was right when he said that it's not so important whether the Lord is on our side, but to be sure we are on the Lord's side. Then we say with courage, "The battle is the Lord's!" A Christ-possessed life is uniquely endowed with power to fight the Lord's battles with Him leading each step of the way.

This is the triumphant story line all through Christian history. The church has never been without persecution, brash or subtle. The bold preaching of Christ and the adventuresome living of His message in all of life have consistently brought stern resistence and cruel rejection. From Pentecost to the present, the martyrs and heroes of the faith have suffered for what they believed. But never alone. The unseen Friend was there.

The Book of Acts is really the biography of that Friend at work through His friends. No prison could exclude Him, no stoning elude Him, no angry mob evict Him, no hatred expunge Him. He was with Peter before the Sanhedrin to give him boldness and with him on a tanner's roof in Joppa pressing him beyond the Judaic to the Gentile world. He was the Lord of Paul's Damascus road and Lord of the Troas road and a call to evangelize Europe. Persecution in Philippi and Thessalonia was sustained in the knowledge that it was better to be in difficulty with the Lord than anywhere else without Him. Resurrection resiliency and the Lord's indwelling power never left Paul. He was constantly in trouble and never without Christ. The Lord's night visits and daily companionship brought courage. "Do not be afraid, but speak, and do not keep silent; for I am with you . . ." (Acts 18:9–10).

What more do any of us need to know? Paul's question can be answered with assurance. "If God is on our side, who can ever be against us?" (Rom. 8:31, TLB). Karle Wilson Baker was right: "Courage is fear that has said its prayers." And prayer is the cumulative expression of friendship with our Lord.

It has been the unique combination of hearing and doing, belief and action, conviction and confrontation that has kept Christians in trouble through the ages. During the ministry of our Lord, people were astonished by what He did as much as by what He said. And He called His followers to build the houses of their lives on hearing and doing. We are meant to be free and open channels to hear His commands and act with obedience. "Therefore," He said, "whoever hears these sayings of Mine, and does them, I will liken him to a wise man who built his house on the rock: and the rain descended, the floods came, and the winds blew and beat on that house; and it did not fall, for it was founded on the rock" (Matt. 7:24–25).

Jesus astonished people by calling for action. We cannot read his challenge to the disciples without reflecting on the fact that it came true. The disciples did astonish the world. Hearing and doing the Master's message distinguished them. I am writing this and you are reading today because they did more than believe in love—they loved; they did more than wring their hands over sin— they preached Christ crucified, alive, and powerful to save; they did more than comfort people—they communicated the Gospel and were its best examples; they didn't write books about spiritual healing—they healed people;

they did more than analyze the discouraging statistics of church membership—they got next to a sick and suffering world and introduced people to Christ; they didn't hold symposiums and endless conferences on social action— they confronted traditions, laws, and customs whenever those restraints debilitated people; they didn't talk about sacrifice—they sacrificed their time, energy, conveniences, careers, and lives so that the world could know that Jesus was Lord. William Temple puts it directly: "The ultimate truth is not a system of propositions grasped by perfect intelligence but a personal Being apprehended by love."

All this leaves us with questions about how we are living this final Beatitude. The temptation is to condemn ourselves if, at the moment, we are not under some persecution because of what we believe. That is to begin at the wrong end. Our first step is to make a "hearing and doing" commitment to Christ. Tell Him that you are ready and willing to follow Him and live His Lordship in every facet of your personal and social life. Remember He is our friend in everything and will lead us.

In our church here in Hollywood, we have called our people to the seven dynamics of contemporary discipleship. We found it both helpful and necessary to articulate the biblical message about what it means to follow Christ today. One aspect is impossible without all the rest.

1. *An unreserved commitment to Christ as Savior and Lord.* That means that we surrender all that we are and have to His complete control.
2. *Daily Bible study and prayer.* It is impossible to grow in friendship with the Lord and receive His guidance without persistent study of the Scriptures and prayer

for marching orders in living out wnat we've stud-
ied.

3. *Tithing.* Until the Lord controls our money and
resources, He will have little sway over our hearts.
Giving the first 10 percent to the Lord's work
involves us in His adventure and breaks the mam-
mon membrane around our wills.

4. *Involvement in weekly worship and some extensive study
to love the Lord with our minds.* All Christians are
called into ministry. The local parish is the seminary
of the laity for in-depth preparation to share our
faith, minister in human need, and follow Christ in
changing the structures of society.

5. *Willingness to witness.* The fruit of one Christian is
another. We were born again to reproduce our faith
in others. We cannot stay alive in vital communion
with Christ without introducing others to Him.

6. *Participation in a small covenant group out in the world.*
We all need a small band of fellow-adventurers with
whom we can share our needs, discern the next step
in being faithful and obedient to Christ, and be
accountable in both hearing and doing.

7. *Extend the Kingdom to the needs of society.* The Lord of
all life leads His people into specific areas of society
where the needs of people are denied, the Gospel
contradicted, or the rule of Christ needs to be
expressed. Every Christian should be involved in at
least one area of involvement with the lost, lonely,
hurting people of the world.

The exciting thing about this sevenfold delineation is
that people have taken it seriously. Many have been led
into difficult and challenging areas of ministry. And it's in

these that Christ's friendship comes alive. The kingdom of heaven is theirs and problems are matched with Christ's power.

Now you can see why I want you to meet my Friena. The eighth Beatitude is impossible to live without the one who spoke it so long ago on the Mount of Beatitude. Trying to live Christ's message without His companionship is impossible. Life will have its tension, tragedies, and excruciating problems. The greater the needs, the deeper our friendship will grow. That is the reason we can be happy, truly blessed, regardless of what happens to or around us.

As a man who had come to know the liberating friendship of Christ put it, "With a friend like that, I can dare anything!"

I
BELIEVE
IN
YOU

10

*"You are the salt of the earth . . .
You are the light of the world."*
MATTHEW 5:13–14

I will never forget when I first heard the four most powerful words a person can say to another. They changed my life. I can remember the occasion as if it happened yesterday.

I was a frightened seventeen-year-old speech student, waiting in the wings of an auditorium to compete in the finals of a national oratorical contest. My future education and development hung on the results. I shook inside with anxiety. Pacing back and forth, I rehearsed in my mind the lines of my carefully prepared oration.

Then suddenly there was someone standing beside me. It was John Davies, my coach and inspiring teacher who had helped me find courage and confidence so often in my high school years. He turned me around, put his hands on my shoulders, looked me in the eye, and said the four esteem-building words, "I believe in you!" With that ringing in my heart, I went out to win the contest and an opportunity to go to college.

Through the years, these four words have been spoken when I needed them most. In times of challenge, of self-doubt, of opportunity, the Lord has given me friends who have dared to say, "I believe in you!" The words have turned fear into hope, uncertainty into courage, and anxiety into confidence.

It's one thing to have a friend say that, but it's all the more liberating to hear the Lord tell us that He believes in us. When the Savior of the world looks us in the eye and says, "I believe in you!" we know that anything is possible.

After Jesus had finished His description of the blessed life He had come to model and enable, I am sure the disciples signaled on their faces their wonderment that He had congratulated them for having such qualities as He had enumerated in the Beatitudes. "He's not talking about the likes of us!" they must have said to each other. That's why He went on to drive home that indeed He did mean what He said. They were the blessed who were now entrusted with the awesome power of influence.

I am convinced that any authentic consideration of the Beatitudes must include Jesus' startling commendation and commissioning of the disciples as salt and light of the world. It was an eloquent, courage-building way of saying, "I believe in you!"

My thesis is this: Jesus infused esteem in the disciples by telling them He believed in them so that they could be people who could say, "I believe in you!" in the world in which they would spread the Gospel. They were Jesus' strategy for changing the world. The same is true for us today. The Lord believes in us even when we don't believe in ourselves. He shakes us out of self-deprecation by telling us that He trusts us to be communicators of salt and light in a bland and dark world. We are the Lord's influential people.

The other day, a man called me with a very generous offer. "I want to put you in touch with some very influential people." "Isn't everyone?" I asked. "No, I mean I want you to meet some really important people," he said persistently. "Isn't everyone?" I asked. "You don't understand," he said impatiently. "These people can open doors for you!" Again my response was, "Can't everyone?"

I appreciated the man's desire to help me, and I am thankful for what people in positions of power have done to encourage me through the years, but the man was missing the significance of his own and everyone's influence.

And yet, the more I reflected on the man's offer, the more I realized that he had given me the three dimensions of influence entrusted to every Christian. We are all important as salt and light; we all have influence to help people find life as it was meant to be; and we all can be door-openers to help others step over the threshold to eternal life.

You are an influential person! Do you believe in your awesome power? Christ does. Everyday, in hundreds of ways, you and I are influencing people about what it means (or does not mean!) to live the abundant life in Christ. If the people of our lives had to write a definition of Christianity from what they see and hear from us, what would they write? Our influence is either positive or negative. People are reading the signals all the time. What kind of salt and light have we been?

People and their needs are our agenda. Our faith, expressed in the eight happy dimensions of the Beatitudes, is to pack a wallop on others. Everything Jesus gives us is for our influence on others. When we settle that, life becomes blessed, indeed! We were meant to have impact, influence, and inspiration in the lives of the people we touch.

When Jesus called the disciples the salt of the earth, He was first of all giving them an affirming image of value, vitality, and viability. All three are implied, as a study of salt at that time reveals. Salt was used to pack fish, as the fishermen among the disciples knew. All the disciples knew that salt was very valuable. In fact, the word for salary comes from the wages of a "sack of salt" paid to Roman soldiers: *sal*—salt; *salarus*—salary. Salt was also used beneath the tiles of an oven. But the main use of the precious commodity was to season and preserve food. Jesus' implied message is that our influence is to pervade, permeate, purify, and preserve. We are to be combatants against blandness and dullness. It is quite a revolution of images to think of ourselves as the zest and flavor of the world. But like salt, our influence is to be inadvertent. We are to bring out the essential qualities of others. No one can at the same time draw attention to himself and make others great.

Jesus goes on to disturb us with the challenge that we can lose our savor. The Greek verb which records Jesus' words, "If salt loses its savor," derives from a word meaning "dull," "sluggish," "foolish." The same word is used by Paul in Romans 1:22, "Professing themselves to be wise, they became foolish." When used for persons, it means foolish; when used for salt, it implies insipidness. It is interesting to note that when a Jew became apostate, part of his restitution was to lie down on the threshold of the door to the synagogue and have people walk on him. He would say, "Trample on me who am salt which has lost its savor." We wonder if Jesus was building on this custom. Little matter—our concern is for how the salt regains its savor. "Salt is good, but if the salt loses its saltiness, how will you season it? Have salt in yourselves, and have peace with one another," Jesus said at another time (Mark 9:50). The passage helps us with the Sermon on the Mount passage.

I am convinced that Christ is the salt of our lives so that we can be the salt of the earth. This is implied: all that we are to be to others, He first is to us. Each of the qualities of the Beatitudes is part of Christ's portrait. All are part of the seasoning of our influence. The Lord was preparing a new creation to be a distinctly different, new breed of humanity. They were to be a model for the world. And He would be the source of renewal and refurbishment for them. In fact, the disciples did lose their savor after the crucifixion and were salted again by the indwelling Christ.

While the disciples were still pondering the "I believe in you!" impact of that, Jesus topped His own metaphor. "You are the light of the world. A city that is set on a hill cannot be hidden. Nor do they light a lamp and put it under a basket, but on a lampstand, and it gives light to all who are in the house. Let your light so shine before men, that they may see your good works and glorify your Father who is in heaven" (Matt. 5:14–16).

Light and truth were synonyms in the Hebrew mind. Jesus declared himself the light of the world in one of His great "I am" statements. His disciples were to be nothing less. Again Jesus is building on the Beatitudes. The blessed are blessed to be a blessing in the world. The term *world* in Scripture implies the realm of the unredeemed, rather than the planet earth in the galaxies of the universe. It is the same world into which God sent His only Son to be light. The disciples' world would broaden after the resurrection and Pentecost. Any area of life, any person, any nation was part of the world in which they were to let their light shine.

Note that Jesus quickly connects light with works: "Let your light shine so that men may see your good works." I think that means words and action. The truth we share illuminates the reason for the good works we do. There's no escaping it: Christ has called us to follow His example and be His examples by what we say and do.

It is helpful to note that there are two words for "good" in Greek. One is *agathos*, meaning good in quality, and the other is *kalos*, implying attractiveness, winsomeness, vitality. *Kalos* is used to translate Jesus' Aramaic word. A good work in that context is one that communicates esteem and affirmation. What we do for people is to prepare them to behold the light of truth which motivated the act. We want people to look to us and wonder why we are the way we are, and then beyond us to the Light of the World flashing in us. The world has a right to expect radiance, warmth, and illumination from us. The example of an exciting life, coupled with winsome witness about its source, and actions which prove its reality are an impelling combination.

Robert Louis Stevenson recorded a childhood incident

in his diary. He was seated by a window at nightfall, watching a lamplighter light the street light below. His nurse came into the room and asked him what he was doing. "I am watching a man make holes in the darkness," he replied. Not a bad description of our calling.

The Lord's illustrations about a city set on a hill and a light under a basket (bushel or peck measure) drove home His belief in His disciples' power of influence, which He did not want them to depreciate. Anyone who has traveled in Palestine late at night knows the source of Jesus' metaphor. I drove to Tiberias from Tel Aviv last summer at midnight and was struck again by the vivid, undeniable lights of hilltop villages.

The lamp under a basket would have had immediate implication for the disciples. In the one-room homes of ancient Palestine, light was given by a saucerlike lamp filled with oil and a floating wick. It was usually placed on a protruding stone built into the wall, called a lampstand. At night, when the family retired or left the house for a time, the lamp was placed under a basketlike peck measure which would keep the light burning low or put it out entirely because of the diminished oxygen.

The Lord's followers caught the point, and so do we. We are left to wonder about the bushels under which we hide our lights. What is it for you and for me? What lowers the brightness or puts out the light? Or what stands in the way of people seeing Christ's light burning in us? For some, it's our personalities, which need Christ's transformation; for others, it's privatism, which keeps us from sharing our faith; for still others, it is simply lack of loving concern. The Psalmist reminds us of our calling. "Let the redeemed of the Lord say so!" (Ps. 107:2).

A woman who had been healed of a dreaded disease through a new method of treatment gave me an unsettling illustration. After she had talked about her healing, she said, "What if I were at a party and someone suffering from the disease from which I've just been cured asked me to share the treatment that saved me? Wouldn't it be the height of ingratitude if I told him I never talked about it because it was too personal? In the same way many Christians hide their lights under a bushel."

We have been given the secret of true happiness. The Lord has come to us down the corridor of our crises when we've cried out, "Help me!" He has comforted us with forgiveness when we've prayed the three words that spell happiness. Out of love, he has given us the two keys to unlock the abundant life. The consuming passion for righteousness He has desired from us He has inspired in us. Mercifully, He has felt our pain in His heart so that we could become the merciful people who empathize and communicate identifying love. He has healed our heart-eyes so that we can see our abject need and His adequacy and then dilated our vision to see the wonder of life, people, and the world. The original, initiating peacemaker died on the cross to give us peace and make us first-steppers. And He's been our friend in all of life's struggles—all so that we could join Him in the ministry of reconciliation.

Listen to Him in the depth of your soul: "I believe in you!"

Read these other books by Lloyd John Ogilvie—

THE BUSH IS STILL BURNING
The Christ Who Makes Things Happen in Our Deepest
Needs

Lloyd Ogilvie asked this question of people across the
country:
*What is the one thing which causes you the greatest difficulty in
your daily living? State your deepest need.* The answers he
received were not surprising: fear, insecurity, loneliness,
disillusionment, guilt, boredom, worry, anxiety, grief,
lack of direction, lack of insight. . . . All of us struggle
with one or more of these, even though we believe in
God.
    Why? Because most of us stumble around with a
concept of God which is vastly inadequate, says Dr.
Ogilvie. We need to discover a new God—the true God
who is present and powerful in our lives today. *The Bush
Is Still Burning* is his eloquent testimony to that God, the
One who is actively involved in our deepest struggles and
whose presence is the answer to our deepest needs.
    This is the God who revealed himself as "I Am" in the
ancient experience of Moses at the burning bush. It is this
same God who revealed more and more of himself
through Jesus Christ, through the many affirmations
Jesus made beginning with the words "I Am":

• "I am the bread of life."—John 6:35
• "I am the light of the world."—John 8:12
• "I am the witness concerning myself."—John 8:18
• "I am the good shepherd."—John 10:11
• "I am the true vine."—John 15:1

These and many other revelations of the true nature of God explode out of their verbal containers. For these are word-pictures Jesus has chosen to bring God's power close to the hidden sources of pain in our lives.

Most of us have given up on one struggle or another, Dr. Ogilvie says, "because we have painted ourselves into a corner of impossibility. We can't imagine that things will change."

It is into this seemingly hopeless situation that God has entered someone's life—over and over, century after century. The bush is still burning, Dr. Ogilvie declares. The experience of a new divine reality is still ours to discover.

WHEN GOD FIRST THOUGHT OF YOU
The Full Measure of Love As Found in 1, 2, 3 John

What would life be like if we really *could* become all God intended when he first thought of us?

The Three Letters of John, says Dr. Ogilvie, contain the penetrating, life-changing truths that will help us rediscover and hold onto the exciting Christian life we first experienced at conversion.

Point by point, Dr. Ogilvie illuminates John's message and translates it into timely, down-to-earth advice for handling our lives as growing Christians:

- How to overcome self-doubt
- How to receive the most from our prayers
- How to use our imagination creatively
- How to reconcile differences of opinion
- How to make Christian decisions
- How to get the best from each stage of life.

But this is much more than a "how to" book. In addition to those specifics, you will find it a moving, living, breathing personal account and interpretation of God at work in each of us. "Claim what is yours," urges Dr. Ogilvie—a life of unlimited potential, spiritually enriched by a vital personal relationship with Christ.

Here are thirty chapters, each of which can be read in less than ten minutes. Read one each day for a month, think about the ideas and experiences Dr. Ogilvie shares, and open your own life to the revolutionary changes God can make. Then read those chapters again, many times, for the insights you can receive are almost inexhaustible and will help keep you growing more and more . . . to be the person God saw *when He first thought of you*.

DRUMBEAT OF LOVE
The Unlimited Power of the Spirit As Revealed in the Book of Acts

Like a drumbeat—

That's how Dr. Ogilvie describes his experience of Christ's love. "In times of challenge and adventure the beat quickens. When difficulties surround me . . . I am never left on my own. If I drift into self-dependence, the beat slows and becomes faint. When I dare to trust the Spirit unreservedly, the beat returns in full force."

In *Drumbeat of Love* Dr. Ogilvie presents the biography of the persistent drummer—the indwelling Christ. The text he interprets is the Acts of the Apostles, and the insights he shares will stir Christians everywhere who are tired of dull, "business as usual" living.

"The astounding, invigorating dynamics of the Holy Spirit have never been more present and available than now," declares Dr. Ogilvie. "That's why a study of the Book of Acts is crucial on God's agenda for our time. This amazing book of Scripture could well be entitled the Acts of the Holy Spirit. It is his story. . . . The fast-moving account leaves us breathless and disturbed. Here is life as God intended it to be lived, and the Church as he envisioned it to be as a channel of power."

In *Drumbeat of Love* Dr. Ogilvie calls on his wide ministry and personal experience to draw significant and striking parallels to our contemporary situation. As he illuminates those qualities and acts of the Holy Spirit which electrified people of the first century, you will experience a "you are there" involvement that dynamizes the all-pervading theme—the urgent imperative for receiving the Holy Spirit and letting Him flow through us.

What the Church needs today, says Dr. Ogilvie, is new fire for renewing the bold witness to Christ's love. We can be ignited and kept burning when we learn to listen for the drumbeat . . . and respond.

LIFE WITHOUT LIMITS
The Message of Mark's Gospel

Life Without Limits offers you a moving rediscovery of Jesus Christ and his triumphant adequacy, an arresting and exciting affirmation of Mark's purpose: to present Jesus of Nazareth as the Messiah, the Son of God, the Savior of all people, through whom God's limitless power is available to all. "Mark really believed that a personal relationship with Christ would result in the same power he dramatized so vividly in the lives of people who met him during his ministry. The same is true for us," says Dr. Ogilvie.

Each chapter of *Life Without Limits* is an exposition of part of Mark's Gospel—some dealing with a few verses, others catching the sweep of Mark's thought over larger portions. Scripture to be covered is designated so as to be helpful in planning personal daily devotions or for use as resource material for small groups.

Life Without Limits is a book born of need . . . of the longing for a sense of direction and life-fulfillment that all of us feel at one time or another. Written in the aftermath of the trauma of Waterate, it answers an equally intense need in an atmosphere haunted by the specter of economic disintegration, ecological deterioration, and world unrest. Dr. Ogilvie communicates Mark's message with contemporary application and illistrations for living the adventure of the new life in Christ today—to help us all "catch the drumbeat for today's adventure in discipleship."

LET GOD LOVE YOU
The Christian Life Style As Seen Through Paul's Letter to Philippian Believers

"Learn to let God live you, and prepare for possibilities you've never imagined!" says Dr. Ogilvie.

God has promised us limitless power to love and care for people—and to joyfully accept their love in return. The Apostle Paul expressed this open secret centuries ago in a letter written to the Christian believers in the city of Philippi. Now in this series of brief, daily devotionals, Lloyd Ogilvie makes the Letter to the Philippians come alive with all its original creative force, and shows its exciting implications for the Christian who is living in contemporary society.

Equally valuable as a guide for personal meditation or as a resource for group study, *Let God Love You* can be a catalyst for discovery, a source of new insight into the dynamics of the Christian life style. "You may want to join the chorus of life-affirming, structure-transforming saints who can sing triumphantly, 'Bother us, we can cope . . . through Christ.'"